A Sourcebook of Income Tax Law in Tanzania

Luoga F. D. A. Makinyika

DUP (1996) LTD.

Published in Tanzania by:
DUP (1996) LTD.
P.O. Box 35182
Dar es Salaam
TANZANIA

ISBN 9976-60-323-1

TABLE OF CONTENTS

AUTHOR'S NOTE

This sourcebook has been written for the sole purpose of guiding students of Tanzanian tax law in the study of the income tax law. Taxing statutes are very fluid. They are subject to frequent yearly changes. As such, this sourcebook is subject to annual reviews. While the sourcebook attempts to address to the interests of tax law practitioners and other practitioners, it does not delve deeper in the most advanced and complex aspects of taxation, particularly relating to intricate corporate finance and tax implications thereof. These are the subject of a next publication which is under preparation.

Luoga, F.D.A.M.
Senior Lecturer in Law
Faculty of Law
University of Dar es Salaam

1

HISTORICAL, LEGAL AND THEORETICAL BACKGROUND

DEFINITION OF TAX

There is no legally formulated definition of the terms "tax" or "taxation." The Oxford dictionary defines a "tax" to mean:

> A *compulsory* contribution to the support of government levied on persons, property, income, commodities, transactions etc, now at a fixed rate mostly proportionate to the amount on which the contribution is levied[1].

This definition as Tiley[2] correctly observes, tells very little apart from the fact that taxes are compulsory. Tiley notes three major weaknesses in the above definition. First, the definition limits the purpose of taxation to the support of government. This is not wholly true since taxes are known to be levied with a non-revenue object such as the use of customs duties to protect domestic industry and the use of taxes to discourage certain habits, for example, the heavy taxation on tobacco and cigarettes which

---

[1] (emphasis added)

[2] Tiley, J. *Revenue Law*, 3rd ed., (London: Butterworths, 1981) p.2

is intended also to discourage smoking. Second, the above definition gives an irrelevant description of the tax base, that is tax is levied on persons, property, income, etc.

Third, it gives undue emphasis on proportionate taxation. The tax can be exacted at progressive rates which are now considered the most appropriate in achieving vertical equity in taxation.

Tiley contends that, not only that taxes are compulsory, but they are also imposed by the legislature, levied by a public body and that taxes are intended for public purposes.[3] In line with Tiley's reasoning, the *Encyclopaedia Britannica* defines "taxes" to mean:

> "Compulsory levies on private units for general governmental purpose"[4]

Even this definition which accommodates Tiley's observations and is comparatively much wider in scope and less restrictive is still insufficient and perhaps outlived its applicability. The changing socio-economic environment has forced many taxing authorities to develop new tax strategies. Recently there has been a significant shift designed to eliminate the element of compulsion in taxation. For example, the governments have introduced the method of collection of revenue through national lotteries.[5] There is little difference between a person who contributes to the support of the government by compulsorily paying the development levy, income tax or a sales tax and a person who contributes to the support of the government by buying lottery tickets. The difference is even insignificant between the buyer of a lottery ticket and a person who buys a revenue stamp. Between the two persons the only visible difference is that the method of imposing the charge and the "tax head" involves direct compulsion while the method of imposing the charge by luring the public into legalized gambling through the lottery system does not involve direct compulsion. Needless to say, both are taxes. The manner by which the levy is exacted, that is, whether by use of compulsion or otherwise is immaterial. Hence the terms "tax" or "taxation" still begs for a definition.[6]

---

3 Ibid.p. 2

4 Vol. II, 15th ed., p. 584

5 See the National Lotteries Act, 1974 Act No. 24 of 1974

6 See the observation of Duff, J. in **Lawson vs. Interior Tree, Fruit & Vegetable Committee of Directions.** (1931) SCR 357 (can.)

BRIEF HISTORY OF TAXATION IN TANZANIA

Tanzania has had a taxation system according to modern principles since the turn of the century. It was introduced by the European colonial powers which took charge of the administration of the territory. The first colonial administrators to introduce taxation were the Germans. They introduced simple forms of direct taxes such as the 'hut' and 'poll' taxes. These were introduced primarily to force the African population to participate in the money economy and only incidentally to raise revenue. The budgetary expenses of the colonial administration were mostly financed by grants from the imperial government. However, the German period in Tanzania did not have a lasting impact on the country's legal institutions including taxation. This is because they failed to establish effective control of the territory. Between 1884 and 1891 the only German presence in Tanganyika was through the German East Africa Company. It was not until 1898 that a colonial government was established. But even then no effective control was achieved. The colonial government's power was severely limited by lack of staff and money. Further, the technique employed to rule the territory was very militaristic and involved the use of strong and ruthless hand. The history of the Germans in Tanganyika is one of continuous resistance by the people. The end of the first World War in 1919 saw the end of the Germans in Tanganyika. The country was declared a trust territory of the League of Nations and handed over to the British (as trustees on behalf of the League of Nations). It was the latter who established institutions that shaped Tanzania's legal and tax structures.

Income taxation was first introduced by the British in 1940. The first income tax legislation was based on a model Colonial Income Tax Ordinance which was essentially a simplified version of the United Kingdom's tax legislation as it existed in about 1920.

Under the British, income taxation was primarily intended for the European portion of the population. The Africans were taxed through import and excise duties mainly because of their low income and literacy levels.

In 1948 the British created the East African High Commission[7] as a statutory corporation to administer and provide in Kenya, Uganda and

---

[7] See the East African (High Commission) Order in Council, 1947.

Tanganyika (The High Commission Territories) certain inter-territorial services. The Order in Council set up a Legislative Assembly with powers to legislate in certain specified matters. Such legislation would, when enacted override the conflicting Territorial legislation. The specified matters were listed in the Third Schedule to the Order in Council and included in Head 5

> Income Tax - Administration and General Provisions (but not including the rates of tax and allowances).

The High Commission decided to synchronise all the tax legislation in the territories by enacting a single managing Act to deal in respect of the whole of East Africa (excluding Zanzibar) leaving each territory to enact separate legislation dealing with rates and allowances. The East African Income Tax (management) Act, 1952[8] was passed to repeal the territorial Ordinances with retrospective effect to January 1, 1951. Between 1952 to 1958 this Act was amended five times.[9] However, it remained in force until 1958 when the East African Income Tax (Management) Act, 1958[10] was enacted. Thus it was not until 1958 that a stable system was established.

According to the scheme of the 1958 Act the tax was levied on residents of East Africa upon their income from sources within East Africa. Income from sources outside East Africa was taxed to the extent that such income was remitted to and received in East Africa. The income upon which the tax was levied was from almost the same sources as enumerated in section 3(2) on the Income Tax Act, 1973.[11] Luoga discusses *in extenso* the scheme of the 1958 Act in his "Ability to Pay: The Basis for Fair Income Taxation in a Developing Country."[12]

---

[8] Act No. 8 of 1952

[9] By East African Income Tax (Management) (Amendment) Acts No. 2 of 1954; (No. 2) Act, No. 14 of 1954; No. 11 of 1955; No. 8 of 1956; and No. 4 of 1958.

[10] Act No. of 1958

[11] Act No. 33 of 1973

[12] *L.L.M.* Thesis, 1988 at the University of Queens, Ontario, Canada

The 1958 Act remained in force until 1971 when the East African Income Tax (Management) Act, 1971[13] was enacted. The latter was short-lived because of the immediate breakdown of the East African Community thereafter. The Income Tax Act, 1973 repealed and replaced the 1971 Act. However, in many respects it is a carry-over of the previous legislation, unfortunately, with some endemic distortions rather than improvements. It is a brief legislation which attempts to achieve a gargantuan task of providing for every aspect of income taxation and apparently, bursting its runs in the process. Luoga (*supra*) attempts an analysis of the Income Tax Act, 1973 in the light of its fairness to taxpayers as well as its effectiveness as a socio-economic tool.

THEORETICAL CONCEPTS OF TAXATION

The often asked question is the need for taxation in society. The classical answer to this question is that taxation is a handmaid for raising revenue to meet governmental expenditure. Imperatively the government has to provide social services, maintain law and order, ensure defence and a horde of other undertakings which the free market cannot provide or which the state feels are better provided by itself - for example, health services and education. The responsibility for the existence and functioning of the government falls on every citizen who must contribute to sustain the government. In practice, however, whether taxes are raised to meet government expenditure or not is of no essence. From the classical point of view, citizens cannot demand from the government benefits equivalent to the taxes they have paid.

In modern times the theories and functions of taxation have been widely and broadly discussed. It is argued that it is impossible to regard taxes as merely a means of obtaining revenue since it may, and is, often used for more specific purposes such as discouraging the use of alcohol or purchase of cigarettes, or as an inducement to production for the market as opposed to subsistence.

Classification of Taxes

Beam and Laiken[14] point out that taxes can be classified in a number of different ways. It may be classified on *the basis of the tax* with the name

---

[13] Cap. 24 of the Community Laws

[14] Beam, R.E. & Laiken, S.N. *Introduction to Federal Income Taxation in Canada*, (Ottawa: CCH Canadian Limited, 1985) pp. 3-4

of the tax reflecting to some extent the tax base or what is to be taxed. For example:

a) A head tax is in essence a tax on the existence of a particular type of taxpayer such as a levy of T.Shs. 200/= paid by all individuals over the age of 18 years;

b) An income tax as the title implies, is a tax on the income of the taxpayer and is exemplified by a tax on the income of individuals or corporations;

c) A wealth tax, such as a tax on capital gains or succession duties, is a tax on the accumulated capital of a taxpayer;

d) A commodity tax is essentially a tax on the consumption of the commodity subject to tax as is the case of a sales tax;

e) A user tax such as a toll for a bridge or road is a tax on the use of a facility or service;

f) A tariff is a tax or duty usually imposed on imported goods to increase the price of such goods relative to domestic goods;

g) A transfer tax is a tax on the value of property transferred from one owner to another as is the case on the transfer of land under certain conditions;

h) A value added tax, as the name implies, is a tax on the increase in value of a commodity created by the taxpayer in moving it from one stage of production or distribution to another.

Another method of classifying taxes is by *the incidence of the tax* which determines the taxpayer who ultimately bears the tax. The incidence of a direct tax is on the initial payer of the tax. For example, the burden of the individual income tax is on the individual who pays the tax. On the other hand, the incidence of an indirect tax is not on the initial payer of the tax, but is on someone else. A sales tax imposed at the manufacturer's level is an example of such an indirect tax.

Taxes can also be classified by *the nature of the tax levy.* A proportional tax is levied at a constant percentage of the income of the payer of the tax. A good example, is the flat rate of tax on corporations in respect of profits and gains made. A progressive tax is levied at an increasing percentage of the income of the payer as is the case for personal income tax. Similarly, a regressive tax is levied at a decreasing percentage of the income of the payer. A sales tax is considered to be a regressive tax to the extent that those with higher incomes spend a lower proportion of that income on the item subject to the sales tax.

Objectives of Taxation

An appraisal of a tax system must be predicated on a widely accepted set of goals or objectives that the nation is seeking, and on a knowledge of the potential role that a tax system can play in the achievement of these goals. Every tax jurisdiction can have a set of objectives which may be different from those in other jurisdictions. But there are several objectives which at least every tax system seems to seek.

a) ***Need for Revenue***

In ancient times taxes were mostly for financing wars. The very existence of a nation requires that its citizens, through their government, must be able to depend themselves against aggressors, and maintain law and order. In recent times governments have taken more responsibilities. In addition to defence and maintenance of law and order, governments provide a wide range of public services. The number, size and coverage of government programmes has increased tremendously. This trend has emphasised the need for expanding sources of revenue in order to finance government expenditure. There are several sources of government revenue. These are basically the non-tax sources and the tax sources of which the latter have gained prominence due to disadvantages which arise from reliance on the non-tax sources as briefly discussed below.

Non-tax sources include the printing of money, borrowing and government sponsored gambling. The creation of currency is a method of financing government expenditure which may be very attractive because of two reasons. First, printing money is comparatively cheaper than borrowing as it does not entail payment of interest and indebtedness. Second, this method does not have the administrative costs involved in the collection of taxes and is also a low profile method of raising revenue than direct taxation and it appears to be less painful to taxpayers than raising the tax rates. However, experience has shown that an increase in money supply to finance government expenditure leads to inflationary pressures in terms of the general price levels. It could be argued that creation of currency is in itself a tax since on the one hand it increases the government's purchasing power while on the other hand, due to the effects of inflation and given a constant income, it decreases the taxpayer's purchasing power. Inflation has been described as "the most unjust and capricious form of taxation."[15]

Government borrowing has been an attractive method of financing government expenditure. It is often relied upon to finance deficit budgets, to ensure a sufficient supply of funds for government expenditure throughout the year, to retire previously incurred debt as it matures, to finance large and costly projects and for many other purposes. This method is frequently criticised on the ground that it shifts the burden of the present government's expenditure to future generations who must pay off both the interest and principal of the debt.

Lastly, government sponsored gambling, such as, national lotteries have become an increasingly popular means of raising revenue. As observed earlier this is also a type of taxation which usually turns out to be highly regressive.

The tax sources include all the taxes, indirect or direct such as the personal income tax, excess profits tax, capital gains tax, estate duty, sales tax, excise taxes, customs duties, road tolls, development levies, registration fees and the like.

b) *Mobilisation of Capital for Capital Formation*

To forge economic development, a country must possess sufficient capital for purposes of investment. In this regard, taxation plays the role of mobilising and accumulating capital from the general public and concentrating the same to the disposal by the government through investments in enterprises that are considered to be of high economic

---

[15] Warren Grover & Frank Iacobucci (eds) *Materials on Canadian Income Tax*, 6th ed., (Don Mills, Ontario: Richard De Boo Publishers, 1985: p. 89)

priority. Taxation collects the residue of income from individuals whose purchasing power is thereby reduced. Individual savings are thus transferred to the government "capital accumulation fund." This in a free enterprise system has an effect of debilitating the growth of the private sector of the economy, but, serves a crucial purpose in a centrally planned economy.

c) ***Allocation of Resources***

Taxation can be used to allocate resources to ventures or geographic areas that are considered underdeveloped. For example, by offering liberal expense deductions in respect of agricultural and mining businesses, investors may be attracted to invest in such enterprises. The tax factor, however, should not be emphasised because investment decisions take count of a horde of other factors as well. Also by allowing a tax holiday in the proposed new capital city i.e. Dodoma by the Dodoma Special Investment Area Act, 1989[16] the government attempts to direct resources to that particular geographical location.

d) ***Stabilization of the Economy***

Taxation can be used as a tool for economic stabilisation first as discussed above, through influencing investment patterns and second, as an inducement to market oriented production as opposed to subsistence production. By imposing taxes people are forced to increase production over and above subsistence level in order to find money for paying taxes.

Sometimes it can be used to boost domestic industrial production e.g. by levying high taxes on imports thereby creating more market for domestic goods and services.

e) ***Distribution of Wealth***

In this respect, taxation is used as a means of redistributing wealth, for instance, by taking away from the wealthy and providing services

---

[16] Act No. 7 of 1989

to the people. Often this is achieved through the use of progressive rate structure.

There are many other specific objectives of taxation. Perhaps Fuller makes the best assessment when he says that taxation is a legal maid for all work.[17]

THEORIES OF TAX DISTRIBUTION

A taxation student needs to know why there are different tax strategies. For example, questions such as, who is taxed, what is taxed and how much is taxed cannot be well comprehended without a knowledge of the theories of tax distribution. These are very complex and highly debatable but an attempt is made to introduce the subject in a very simplistic manner.

There are several theories of tax distribution which have been used to select the rates and bases upon which taxation should be levied. The three major theories are the benefit theory of taxation, the sacrifice theory and the ability to pay theory.

The benefit theory rests on the commercial principle that it is only fair to pay for what you get. It emphasises that when someone receives a direct and measurable benefit from the government it is only fair and logical that he should pay for it. This theory seeks to ensure that each individual's tax obligations are as far as possible based on the benefits that he or she receives from the enjoyment of public services.

For example, Hobbes argues that taxes must be proportional to benefits received and the chief benefit is the protection afforded. He observes that:

> For what reason is there, that he which laboureth much, and sparing the fruits of his labour, consumeth little, should be more charged, than he that living idly, getteth little, and spendeth all he gets; seeing the one has no more protection from the commonwealth than the other? But when

---

[17] Fuller, Lon. L. *The Morality of Law*, (New Haven; London: Yale University Press, 1964) p. 166

> the impositions are laid upon those things which men consume, every man payeth equally for what he useth, nor is the commonwealth defrauded by the luxurious waste of private men.[18]

In practice, however, this theory is difficult to apply. It is narrow and atomistic. There are three very fundamental weaknesses of the theory. First, it is not practicable to measure the proportionality of the benefits to income. Second, it is difficult to find an appropriate measurement of the benefits because benefits received can either be measured in terms of benefits received from the government, such as, government services, or benefits received from the economy as a whole through personal consumption. Third, there is, in general, no way in which policy makers can determine individual evaluation of public services, hence, it becomes difficult to determine the relationship between the taxes paid and the marginal benefits received by particular individuals.

The major application of the benefit principle in practice appears to be the justification of differential taxation on those individuals particularly benefited by public service when no re-distributive purpose is desired and it is not possible to charge directly for the services rendered. For example, special taxes on motor vehicles and fuel, pay-roll taxes, water-rates, electricity tariffs etceteras.

The sacrifice theory attempts to determine the burden that rests upon an individual in virtue of his payment of taxes and how much of his or her income remains for purposes of his own subsistence. According to this theory payment of tax is a sacrifice that an individual makes towards the support of the government. The measure of such sacrifice is found in the giving up of enjoyments, that is, giving up a portion of an individual's means (i.e. income) of satisfying wants (i.e. consumption). Practically the sacrifice theory demands that individuals should only pay tax on that portion of income that is spent on luxuries. In other words, the sacrifice should only be in respect of an individual's means over and above subsistence. This theory has often been associated with

[18] See. Thomas Hobbes, *Leviathan* London: Penguin Books Ltd., 1981 p. 217

proportional rates of income taxation.[19] Applicability of this theory is conceptually difficult unless it is expressed in terms of income and consumption.

Inadequacies in the benefit and sacrifice theories of taxation led to the development of the concept of ability to pay. This simply refers to the ability of taxpayers to pay taxes, or as Goode puts it:

> The capacity of paying without undue hardship on the part of the person paying or an unacceptable degree of interference with objectives that are considered socially important by other members of the community.[20]

The theory of ability to pay requires that tax burdens should be distributed according to the individual abilities of taxpayers. Raphael observes that:

> In the distribution of benefits and burdens, differences must be justified by relevant differences in the recipients. Thus it is just to give more money to A than to B, if A is more deserving or if A is more needy; and it is just to give more responsibility to C (or to ask more of him) than D, if C is more able to bear the responsibility or to make the contribution asked. In the absence of any such differences between A and B or C and D, it will be just to treat them equally.[21]

The above definitions explain the theory of ability to pay in simple and easily understandable words. However, in practical terms it has never

---

[19] Perhaps this is because of John Stuart Mill's advocacy. See Mill's testimony in Report of the Tax Commission of 1852 in Weston, S.F. *Principles of Justice in Taxation* (N.Y. AMS Press, 1968) p. 286 - 312.

[20] Goode, R. *Individual Income Tax* Rev, ed., (Washington: The Brookings Institute, 1976) p. 17.

[21] Raphael, D.D. "Taxation and Social Justice" in B.Crick & W.A. Robson (eds) *Taxation Policy* (London: Penguin Books Ltd., 1973) p. 51.

had any definite meaning. For example, the theory does not suggest any base upon which taxes are to be levied. It raises the difficult of trying to translate ability to pay into an actual pattern of tax distribution. That is what should be the measure of a taxpayer's ability and what should be the pattern of distributing the tax burden.[22] To understand the controversies which permeate the three theories of tax distribution it is imperative for a taxation student to understand certain basic concepts as follows.

a) **Tax Unit**

This relates to the question, who is taxed? One of the most difficult problems in formulating tax policy is to find a method of identifying the tax paying unit which best accommodates the ideal of taxing on the basis of ability to pay. There are three possible tax units, namely, the individual, the married couple and the family unit. Tax can be levied either on the individual as is the case with the Tanzanian income tax and the development levy, or on the married couple as was the case under the East Africa Income Tax (Management) Act, 1958; or on the family.

Under the individual tax unit, every individual's tax-paying ability is determined separately and a tax levied on the individual in person. The married couple tax unit requires that husband and wife should be assessed and taxed jointly. There is a general acceptance that the family is the most appropriate unit of taxation. However, there appears to be no harmony on what methods are to be used in determining a family's taxable capacity. Some experts have argued that there is no individual ability to pay but only a family ability. Others have maintained that a family has no ability of its own but possesses a cumulative ability of its members. The first method suggests that income of the whole family should be aggregated and ability measured on the totality of the family income. The second argument suggests that the ability of every member should be determined separately before aggregation. Both arguments appear to be in agreement in one respect. That is, it is inappropriate to tax an individual on his assumed personal ability without considering family circumstances.

---

[22] See Henry Simons, *Personal Income Tax* (Chicago: The University of Chicago Press, 1955) p. 17

b) **Tax Base**

This relates to the question, what is taxed? Choice of a tax base is perhaps the most important yet contentious issue in taxation. There are three competing tax bases, namely, the income base, the expenditure base and the wealth base. But before we look at each of these bases it is imperative to examine what one should look for in a taxation system.

Adam Smith in *The Wealth of Nations*[23] promulgated certain criteria for evaluating taxation systems. He said there are four canons of taxation:

Equity

That is, the subjects of every state ought to contribute to wards the support of the government as nearly as possible in proportion to their respective abilities, i.e. in proportion to the revenue which they respectively enjoy under the protection of the state.

Traditionally equity is divided into two suits:

a) Horizontal equity, which means that those in equal circumstances should pay an equal amount of tax, or similar individuals should be treated similarly. This requires that administrative arrangements should ensure that the tax does not impinge heavily on some transactions while exempting others, and the system ought not to create a bias such that the tax is paid by the honest and those without effective tax advisors or those reluctant to reorganise their affairs so as to minimise their tax liabilities.

b) Vertical equity which is concerned with the burden imposed by the tax rates. This is the principle that those in unequal circumstances should pay different amounts of tax, or persons with different financial capabilities should be treated differently. In distributing the tax burden the rate structure has to ensure that persons with comparatively high income pay more in taxes than those with low incomes.

---

[23] Vols. 1-3, London: Methuen, 1961

Certainty

This simply means that the scope of the tax should be clear. The tax which each individual is bound to pay ought to be certain and not arbitrary. The time of payment, the manner of payment and the amount to be paid, ought all to be clear and plain to the contributor and to every other person.

Convenience

According to this canon every tax ought to be levied at the time, or in the manner in which it is most likely to be convenient for the contributor to pay it. A good example, is the collection of income tax from employees through the PAYE system and the withholding tax system on dividend and interest income earned by residents of Tanzania as well as on other payments made by residents to non-residents.[24]

Economy

That is, every tax ought to be so contrived as both to take out and to keep out of the pockets of the people as little as possible, over and above what it brings into the public treasury of the state.

Adam Smith's canons have in modern times been modified into the following major headings.

Social Justice (equity)

That is, taxes imposed should be just. They should be impartial in their application and should be designed to reduce economic inequalities (equality test) treating equals equally and unequals unequally. Also that the tax burden should be relative.

Consistency With Economic Goals

This is seen as efficient allocation and full employment or utilisation of resources, rising living standards and economic stability. Taxes should restrict private spending during inflation and expand it during depression. Also that they should interfere least with incentives and conversely, stimulate the will to work and entrepreneurship.

---

[24] See sections 36 and 34 of the Income Tax Act, 1973 (*supra*)

Easy of Administration

An ideal tax is that which can be administered at reasonable cost to both the government and the taxpayer, which cannot be easily evaded or avoided through legal loopholes and subterfuges, and which is simple to compute, easy to understand in terms of its concepts, assessed on an easy base, levied at moderate rates and payable in a convenient manner.

Revenue Adequacy

That is, the tax strategy adopted should be capable of raising the required funds in the manner best suited to finance the government.

Having examined what one should look for in a taxation system, it is now appropriate to discuss the competing tax bases.

i) **The Income Tax Base**

It is very difficult to define what income means. There has never been any consistent definition of income. Income in the sense of recurring cash receipts from a regular source or a number of definite and ascertainable sources is the practical base on which income taxation is built.

In the United States of America income includes gains, profits and income from salaries, wages or compensation for personal services, or return derived from capital or from labour and capital combined, in whatever form realised.

In Canada income is defined to mean income as determined by statutory rules.

In the United Kingdom there is no statutory definition of income. Income is simply identified with sources contained in the schedules of charge.

More often than not, in the tax laws of many tax jurisdictions, income is defined in terms of sources. Hence the source concept of income.

The source concept of income, however, does not provide an ideal base for taxation because if an amount cannot be fitted into a schedule, and is not classified as emanating from a specified source, then it is outside the definition of income for taxation purposes. For example, gifts, inheritances and windfalls not being from a specified source or arguably any source, are not included in income. Capital gains have for a long time been excluded because they are part of the source (the increase in its value) and therefore capital.

Further, the source definition of income is highly inequitable. It leads to preferential treatment of certain items such as capital gains and exclusion of others such as gifts and bequests from the income tax base. Definitely a shilling will support the same amount of consumption and accumulation irrespective of its source.

The source concept which is based on an agrarian society is outmoded and cannot equitably function in today's sophisticated and complex economic society. For example, since this concept restricts taxation on a realisation and not an accrual basis, in that, it taxes only when a market transaction occurs and it takes a flow of wealth concept which excludes from its scope non-recurrent or unusual forms of income such as imputed income and earned income in kind.

ii) **The Expenditure Tax Base**

This is sometimes referred to as the "consumption tax base." Taxation could be levied on the total value of an individual's consumption expenditure during the course of the year. This is an alternative tax base to income taxation.

An individual's expenditure could be measured by observing what he does with the various cash receipts arising during the course of the year.

For example, suppose a person begins the year with T.Shs. 500/= in cash. He receives T.Shs. 4,000/= in salary, T.Shs. 100/= in dividends and T.Shs. 1,000/= from the sale of shares of stock during the year. Thus the income to be accounted for is T.Shs. 5,600/=. During the year he buys T.Shs. 1,500/= in bounds (investment), repays a debt of T.Shs. 200/= and his bank account at the end of the year is T.Shs. 200/=. The funds unaccounted for are therefore T.Shs. 5,600/= less T.Shs. 1,500/= (expended). The resultant amount of T.Shs. 3,800/= is taken to be his consumption or taxable spending. Exemptions may of course be provided. Thus if the exemption is T.Shs. 1,000/= and the first bracket rate (say the first T.Shs. 1,000/=) is 5% and the second bracket rate (say T.Shs. 2,000/= to 4,000/=) is 10% he would be called upon to pay T.Shs. 230/= in tax.

It should be noted that an expenditure tax is not the same as a sales tax. An expenditure tax like an income tax is based on individual returns and it can have whatever degree of progressivity desired.

It is argued that an expenditure tax is more equitable than an income tax base because the former rates an individual's spending capacity according to the yardstick which he applies to himself. Further, that a progressive expenditure tax falls more heavily than progressive income tax on the wealthy who are financing high levels of consumption out of capital resources. An expenditure tax base brings an end to all conceptual difficulties associated with the income tax base. For example, the income capital receipt distinction could be dispensed with; inflation and depreciation need not be taken into account in the taxation statute because the individual himself will take them into account in making his consumption decisions; and, averaging provisions could be dispensed with *etceteras*. However, so far the only know countries to have experimented the expenditure tax are India and Sri Lanka and have both discarded it due to virtually insurmountable administrative constraints. For instance, to operate smoothly, taxpayers must be inculcated with the habit of keeping bank accounts and should be able to well document their transactions.

iii) **The Wealth Tax Base**

The expenditure or consumption tax base has been criticised on the grounds that it increases the returns on savings and increases the opportunities to amass great wealth compared to the existing tax system. Similarly, the income tax has been criticised as being an inadequate method to tax wealth and is an inefficient way to reduce disparities in wealth between persons.

Briefly, a wealth tax is a tax on a person's total assets minus his liabilities. There are certain accretions that neither income nor expenditure taxes can reach, for example, wealth on which no explicit cash return is earned and which is not spent. This wealth may be held to generate various forms of non-money income such as the imputed rent on owner-occupied housing, the imputed liquidity income derived from holding cash and amenities derived from owning works of art, antiques and jewellery.

However, this base of taxation has been difficult to apply. Experience from the few developing countries that have attempted to introduce this tax shows that they lack sufficient administrative expertise to successfully levy this tax. Fairness of the tax is undermined by the difficulty of discovering the ownership of intangible assets and their valuation. It is also likely to present a problem to taxpayers who have property, but little or no current income. It forces them to dispose of part of their assets in order to pay tax.

iv) **The Negative Income Tax Concept**

This is a concept which has been recently developed. It involves the replacement of all present welfare and income supplement payments. The assumption is that taxpayers could have a guaranteed annual income. The negative income tax is simply an extension of the current progressive income tax structure which is designed to increase the income of those people whose level of income is below a designated poverty line.

Under the negative income taxation, if the income of the taxpayer exceeds that of the arbitrarily selected "poverty line" it is to that extent taxed normally; if it falls below this line the provisions of the negative income tax come into play. The taxpayer is guaranteed receipt of a basic allowance regardless of earned income. If the taxpayer has some income but less than the poverty line amount, he or she receives the basic allowance and is as well allowed to keep a set proportion of other income.

c) **Rate Structure**

Different strategies have been adopted to achieve the goal of taxing according to ability to pay. Whereas a number of countries have favoured the use of progressive income taxation, other countries have employed proportional income taxation. Others, on purely economic and political considerations, have adopted regressive income taxation. As to which of the different strategies is ideal is a controversial question.

Marginal utility analysts with their principle of diminishing utility of income have argued that ability to pay tax increases faster than increases in income. Therefore, progressive rates should be used as an instrument to effect equitable distribution of the tax burden.

For example, to achieve this objective the Carter Commission[25] in Canada suggested that in determining the rate schedule the parameters should be:

a) The determination of the upper and lower limits to the range over which the proportion of income available for discretionary use;

b) The selection of the basic tax rate (or rate of tax on discretionary income) that yields the desired amount of revenue. (They considered that this would be the maximum marginal rate applicable to income above the upper limit);

c) The selection of the intervening tax brackets between the lower and upper limits that cover roughly equal percentage changes in income; and

d) The selection of intervening tax rates that increase equally between zero and the maximum rate, and apply these rates to the intervening brackets.

However, these parameters, especially the concept of non-discretionary income introduces subjective judgements which is dangerous. Professor Pigou laid down four restrictive tax criteria in formulating rate structures. These are:

a) The tax levy on nil income should be nil

b) The amount of taxation assessed on a smaller income should not be greater than the amount assessed on a larger income

c) The average rate of taxation should not increase for some increases in the amount of income and decrease for other increase, i.e. is progressive for some scales of income and regressive for others; and

d) The total amount of the tax levy should not be greater than the amount of income on which it is levied.

---

[25] The Royal Commission on Taxation, 1962 (Canada). See commentaries in Bucovetsky. & Bird "Tax Reform in Canada - Progress Report," 25 *Nat.* J. 15 and in Bale, "The Individual and Tax Reform in Canada" (1971), 44 *Can. Bar Rev.* 24 at pp. 78 - 79.

Legal traditionalists who still believe that the best tradition of a just law is to provide equal treatment to all have encouraged and defended the use of proportional income taxation. They argue that under a proportional tax everyone who pays is left in relatively the same position in which he was found. There is no attempt to disturb market rewards.

Nevertheless, there has been no rate structure free of value judgements and that achieves the ideal of taxing according to ability on all its four.

THE TAX SYSTEM AND INFLATION

Inflation influences the working of a tax system in several ways which if neglected will distort the anticipated effects of the tax. For example:

a) The ability to defer tax liability and payments is more valuable in times of inflation as the payment will ultimately be made in depreciated shillings. Unless the same ability to defer tax payments is possessed by all taxpayers it is inevitable that inequities will occur.

b) For wage and salary earners who have their income tax deducted at source, commonly occurring excess deduction amounts to interest-free loan to the government. Refund of tax becomes less valuable because it is effected in inflated shillings.

c) The tax draft effect. That is, as taxpayer incomes are increased as part of the inflationary spiral, they drift upwards into higher tax brackets in a progressive income tax rate structure. This drift tends to increase the tax revenue of the government as a percentage of the Gross National Product (GNP) and creates a windfall tax yield for the government without having to undertake the politically unsavoury step of increasing tax rates. The tax drift however causes an increased tax burden on taxpayers given the same real income.

d) Where personal and dependant deductions are given, the value of the same is affected to the extent that these allowances do not keep pace with inflation. Their real value is eroded.

e) Inflation also complicates the determination of business income. During inflation profits determined on the basis of conventional historical accounting methods do not reflect true profits which are materially lower. These same methods, when employed in arriving at net income for income tax purposes can lead to business income being taxed more heavily than intended. When this occurs, the viability of business suffers. "True" retained profits are reduced to below the level needed for continuing operations.

f) Taxation of capital gains is also complicated. Owing to inflationary pressures a taxpayer may find that he has an asset which has appreciated solely because of the general price level increase causing an illusory capital gain.

2

INTERPRETATION OF TAX STATUTES

SOURCES OF TAX LAW

There are three main sources of tax law, namely, taxing statutes, cases and departmental practices.

Statute Law

Tax laws derive from Acts of Parliament which make such laws such as the Income Tax Act (1973, the Customs and Tariff Act (1976), the Export Tax Act (1974), the Stamp Duty Act (1972), the Transfer Tax Act (1967), the Entertainment Tax Act (1970), the Hotel Levy Act (1972), and a lot of other taxing legislation. Complimentary to all these pieces of legislation are the Finance Acts which often amend the various provisions of the taxing statutes or provide for new or additional matters thereto.

Case Law

These are decisions of judicial authorities on matters concerning taxation to which reference is frequently essential. It is important to note, however, that in construing taxing statutes the courts or judicial authorities do not create new law. But, precedents are very important in deciding particular points at issue and also for the principles which may be derived from the interpretation of statutes by judicial authorities, hence case law authority.

Departmental Practice

The day to day application of tax law often gives rise to difficulties and in the absence of case law authority on a particular point, sometimes statements of departmental practice or an interpretation put on a statutory provision as a matter of practice becomes of great importance and assistance.

For example, it is not clear whether the amount of T.Shs. 1,000/= referred to in Section 5(2)(b) of the Income Tax Act (1973) refers to the cumulative value of the benefits or to each benefit received per annum or per each transaction conferring the same. There is no case law authority on the point and the relevant statute is itself of little help. However, the Income Tax Department's practice is to compute the value of such benefits over a period of a year in order to ascertain taxability thereof. Departmental practice however is prone to challenges in courts of law.

THE ESSENCE OF TAX LAW CONSTRUCTION

Often, many words and phrases which are used in taxing statutes either have no technical meaning in law or they simply have no precise meaning in ordinary use.

An example, is the words "profits or gains" of a "business" in the Income Tax Act, 1973. The terms "profits or gains" are not statutorily defined, whereas the term "business" lacks a satisfactory statutory definition. Or, the term "trade" which also lacks satisfactory statutory definition is also difficult to ascertain its meaning in its ordinary usage. Although the term "trade" is widely used and appears common, but as regards its application in tax law it poses problems.

For instance, whether an isolated transaction of purchase and resale of property constitutes a "trade" or whether or particular payment is an "annual payment" i.e. an annuity within the scope of the Income Tax Act are matters which have to be construed. Therefore, due to this lack of precision it has become necessary to define the words or phrases (by practice or precedent) to enable those applying tax law to decide on various taxing matters.

Courts have been playing the role of interpreting the law as laid down in the statutes to give meaning to the words and phrases which in themselves do not have precise meaning. What the courts do in construing taxing statutes is in effect the same as in other statutes, namely, to ascertain the intention of the legislature as it appears from the language it has used.[26]

Basic Principles in Construing Tax Statutes

There are two basic principles in construing taxing statutes.

a) No tax can be imposed on a subject without words in the Act showing clearly the intention to impose tax. Therefore, even where it may be within the spirit of the Act to impose tax on some item no tax would be imposed if the statute is silent or has no clear provision.[27] This principle in Tanzania is also enshrined in the Constitution which by Article 138 prohibits imposition of tax of any kind save by an Act of Parliament.[28]

b) In tax cases the court may ignore the legal position and regard the substance of the matter or the equivalent financial results as was the case in the case of **IRC v. Duke of Westminster.**[29]

---

[26] See the case of IRC Vs. Hinchy (1960) AC 748 where it states the objects of constructing taxing statutes.

[27] A clear example of this principle can be seen in the case of **Cape Brady Syndicate vs. IRC** (1921) 1 KB 64 at 71

[28] The Constitution of the United Republic of Tanzania, 1977. See also Article 99(2) (a) (i) of the Commission. For further judicial authority on this point read the cases of **Coltness Iron Co. vs. Black** (1881) App. Cas. 330; **Ormond Co. Ltd. vs. Betts** (1928) AC 143 at 151; and **Russell vs. Scott** (1948) AC 422 at 433.

[29] (1936) AC 1; see also 14 ATC 77, or 19 TC 490.

General Guidelines in Construing Tax Statutes

Choice of the Method of Interpretation

Choosing the method of interpretation to be followed is usually influenced by the "parade of horribles", that is, the undesirable consequences which may result from adopting an alternative method of construction.

For example in **Jafferali Alibhai v. CIT**[30] the appeal emanated from an Order of the Commissioner of Income tax that 60% of undistributed company income be deemed to have been distributed as dividends.

The commissioner's order was based on section 22(2)(a) of the East African Income Tax (Management) Act, 1958. This provision was not applicable to a public company in which the public is free to participate during the "relevant period." The company was a private company which later on became public (at mid year) and challenged the commissioner's order as being incompetent.

The issue was whether the terms "relevant period" meant throughout the year of income or at any time during such year of income. The commissioner proposed the adoption of the mischief rule of interpretation arguing that the intention of the legislature by enacting section 22(2)(a) was to curb the evil of evasion through capitalisation of income. The contention of the Commissioner was that to hold that the term "relevant period" meant the whole year of income would make nonsense of the provision because a company which was private for 364th days of the year but became a public company on the 365th day would escape the application of section 22.

The argument by the Commissioner in the above case seeks to influence the court to select a method of interpretation favourable to the taxing authority by parading the horror of tax evasion.[31]

The party seeking a particular interpretation of a statute or opposing another will point out to the court the dire consequences of adopting the unwanted interpretation i.e. he presents the court with a "parade of horribles."

---

[30] 3 EATC 328

[31] However, the court in the said case rejected the proposed mischief rule in favour of the ordinary meaning rule because the words of the said provision were clear and unambiguous.

Case Law Examples

In **X v. CIT**[32] the taxpayer in support of his proposed construction of the statute suggested that adoption of another construction would allow the commissioner to make assessments which were arbitrary and fantastically high.

In **Mandavia v. CIT**[33] the counsel for the taxpayer had asked the court to consider the serious consequences which he thought would arise from the interpretation of the statute in question put forward by the Commissioner.

The question involved interpretation of Section 72 of the East African Income Tax (Management) Act, 1958 which the counsel contended that it should have a restricted rather than a general application because it inflicts hardship on the taxpayer. He proposed that the interpretation should be as one in a previous English Statute providing that where a penal statute or a taxing statute is of ambiguous meaning, the construction more favourable to the subject should be adopted.

Position of Collateral Literature

Collateral literature include Bills stating objects and reasons for enacting the statute, the Hansards, Commission reports, *ejusdem generis*. The general position is that such collateral literature cannot be used as a legitimate aid to statutory interpretation.[34]

Case Law Examples

In CIT v. BG[35] the court was concerned with consideration of Commission recommendations which led to the enactment. It held that commission recommendations are not proper guidance to the interpretation of the enactment.

---

[32] 2 EATC 39

[33] 2 EATC 426

[34] Note, however, the position in Tanzania in this regard appears to have been changed by the decision in **Joseph Sinde Warioba vs. Stephen Wassira**, AG Civil Appeal No. 52 of 1996, (Dar es Salaam) (unreported) using the "purposive" approach of appears that the court can read words into a provision of law in order to give effect to the objects which the statute was designed to achieve. Read also, **Kammis Ballrooms Co. Ltd. v. Zenith Investments (Terquay) Ltd.** [1970] 2 All ER 871, at 893 and **Nothman v. Barnet** London Borough Concil [1978] 1 All ER 1243 at p. 1246.

[35] EATC 165 at 169

In **CIT v. D**[36] the collateral literature was a statement of the Attorney General as to the intended scope of the section in issue. The court ruled that the statement was an improper aid in construction.

Comparisons with Foreign Law

Tanzanian tax legislation may at some points be similar to tax legislation in the other countries of the commonwealth. Sometimes consideration is made of interpretation assigned to provisions in the other countries which are in *pari materia* with Tanzanian provisions.

The position is that, where the provisions in question are in *pari materia* i.e. are similar, the interpretation used in foreign provision may provide guidance in construction subject to the differences.

Case Law Examples

In **Ralli Estates Ltd v. CIT**[37] the phrase under consideration was "expenditure wholly and exclusively expended in the production of income." The counsel wanted to rely on an English Statute's interpretation. The wording in the English Statute read "expenditure wholly and exclusively laid out for the purpose of the trade, profession or vocation." The court observed that differences in words used must be handled very carefully. That where the provisions are so different, any comparison may be rendered useless.[38]

In **BJ v. CIT**[39] the taxpayer in support of his claim for a child allowance and an education allowance argued that Section 52 of the East African Income Tax (Management) Act, 1958 should be compared with section 212 of the English Income Tax Act, 1952. The court rejected the taxpayer's argument saying that the statutes were quite different.

In **CIT v. Directors of A.Y. Ltd**[40] it was the commissioner who based his position on the alleged similarity of the English Income Tax Act,

---

[36] 1 EATC 27 at 29

[37] 2 EATC 203 at 232

[38] On this point also see the cases of **TM Bell vs. CIT** 3 EATC 102 at 131; **CIT v. Overland, Co. Ltd.** 3 EATC 307; and **CIT vs. Williamson Diomonds Ltd.** 2 EATC 309

[39] 3 EATC 263

[40] 2 EATC 414

1952 (provisions regarding pension rights of directors and employees) to sections of the East African Income Tax (Management) Act, 1952. The court rejected the commissioner's argument because of significant differences between the statutes.

Administrative Practices

The question here is whether it is legitimate to look at how the tax department has interpreted a particular provision. Courts on certain occasions are asked to look at administrative practices to determine the meaning of a statute. This technique of construction is referred to as "practical construction" and is only used when the practice is in favour of the taxpayer.

Case Law Examples

In **TM Bell v. CIT**[41] the Department of Income Tax had adopted an arrangement of convenience of allowing the practice of filing one memorandum of appeal against several assessments.

The issue was whether it was competent for the appellant taxpayer to file one memorandum of appeal in relation to several assessments.

Section 78 of the East African Income Tax (Management) Act, 1952 provided only for appeal against the assessment. The court held that departmental practice could not be used as a guide to construction. That, however, even though at times courts have admitted departmental practice, it has to be very careful. It is very unsafe to rely on departmental practice.

In **Commissioners for Special Purposes of the Income Tax v. Pensel**[42] the court reasoned that in deciding whether departmental practice has to be taken into account one has to assume that the legislature every time it sits is aware how the law is applied by the tax officers. Therefore, where the term used in a statute is the same as that used by the department it should be inferred that the legislature intended that the interpretation should be like that of the department.

---

[41] 3 EATC 102 at 104-6

[42] (1891) AC 431 at 590-91

Rules For Construing Taxing Statutes

1. *The Strict Construction Rule*

The general rule is that tax statutes must be strictly construed. Strict construction means basically two things:

First, it means the use of the plain meaning approach. That is, one is merely to look at what is clearly said. This rule requires that the courts must have regard to the exact words used in a taxing statute and not suppose any general principle underlying them and remaining unexpressed. As Rowlatt, J. observed in **Kliman v. Winkworth**:[43]

> ... in taxation you have to look simply at what is clearly said. There is no room for any intendment; there is no equity about tax; there is no presumption as to tax; you read nothing in; you imply nothing, but you look fairly at what is said and at what is said clearly and that is the tax.

According to this rule no tax can be imposed on a subject unless the words in the Act of Parliament clearly imposes the tax on him.[44]

Second, it also means the used of the *contra-preferentum* rule. That is, regard is to be had to all the words used without making any addition to them. Where there is ambiguity the taxing statute should be construed in favour of the taxpayer.[45]

In recent times, however, strict construction has come under attack by a trend which favours a more liberal construction aimed at giving effect to the intention of the legislature especially when interpreting anti-avoidance

---

[43] (1933) 17 TC 569 at 572

[44] Other cases on the strict construction rule include **Cape Brady Syndicate. vs. IRC** (*supra*); **Canadian Eagle Oil Co. vs. King** (1946) AC 119 at 140; **CIT vs. Directors of A.Y. Ltd.** (*supra*); **IRC vs. Barclays** (1951) AC 421 at 439; and **Sir George Arnoutoglo vs. CIT** 3 EATC 473 at 500-1.

[45] See the cases of **Mandavia vs. CIT** (*supra*) and **Coutts & Co. vs. IRC** (1913) AC 267 at 281.

provisions because it is impossible for the legislature to foresee and forestall ingenious taxpayer schemes of avoiding tax.[46]

Before the above recent trend the attitude of the East African Court of Appeal can be clearly seen in cases on *"Casus Omissus"* i.e. cases of omission within taxing statutes.

The courts in East Africa although concerned with the spirit of the legislation were, nevertheless, reluctant to fill in gaps which the legislature have left open even with anti-avoidance provisions.

For example, In **CIT v. U**[47] the question involved the construction of the word "public." The commissioner asked the court to construe the word "public" in conformity with the spirit of the provision, i.e. to curb tax-avoidance. The court rejected the proposed liberal construction in favour of strict construction.

In **TM Bell v. CIT**[48] the court was called upon to determine the meaning of the words "shareholder" and "shareholders." The issue was whether the terms could be extended to include executors of a deceased's estate and persons having beneficial interest thereto. The commissioner had assessed executors to income tax on income from distributed dividends. The court held that the words must be construed strictly. It pointed out thus:

> If the person sought to be taxed comes within the letter of the law he must be taxed, however great the hardship may appear to the judicial mind to be. On the other hand, if the crown, seeking to recover tax, cannot bring the subject within the letter of the law the subject is free, however apparently within the spirit of the law the case might otherwise appear to be.[49]

---

[46] Case law favouring liberal construction could be seen in the cases of **Greenberg vs. IRC** (1971) AC 109 at 137; **Ramsay vs. IRC** (1982) AC 300 (HL); and **Furniss vs. Dawson** (1984) 1 All ER 530 (HL).

[47] 2 EATC 1 at 12

[48] (*Supra*)

[49] The court in making that statement quoted Lord Macdermott in the case of **IRC vs. Barclays Banks Ltd.** *(supra)*.

2. ***Considering the Statute as a Whole***

The Act is to be considered as a whole. Sometimes the meaning of a word or phrase in the Act though vague or ambiguous in one place, is clear in another or the two are clear when considered together. Hence sometimes considering the Act as a whole gives a clue as to the meaning of a part.[50]

It is, however, important to note that where there is an irreconcilable conflict, in that, two provisions on the surface appear irreconcilable, each have to be interpreted in a manner which will not negate the other. For example, in **CIT v. J**[51] the issue was whether the Respondent was entitled, in arriving at the figure for his chargeable income, to deduct from his total income the sum of £ 350 which is allowed to be deducted under section 24(1)(a) of the Income Tax Ordinance by any person who in the year preceding the year of assessment had a wife living with or wholly maintained by him. The Commissioner refused to allow the deduction on the strength of section 34(3) within the said Ordinance which provided that:

> when a married woman is not living with her husband each spouse shall *for all the purposes of this Ordinance* be treated as if he or she were unmarried" (emphasis mine).

The commissioner argued that since the wife was not living with the Respondent the words "for all the purposes..." operated to grant an independent status to her and as such the Respondent was not entitled to the claimed deduction. The Respondent taxpayer argued for the expression "living with or wholly maintained by him" in the said section 24 saying that if the commissioner's interpretation would be adopted the said Section 24(1)(a) would be redundant and useless.

The court found that there is an obvious conflict and held that the words "for all purposes" must be read in the context of Section 34(3)(a). That is, they must be read subject to the implied exception in Section 24(1)(a).

---

50 See the application of this rule in construing the word "individual" in **B. vs. CIT** 1 EATC 6. Also read **IRC vs. Herbett** (1913) AC 326 at 332.

51 1 EATC 80

3. *Words of the Statute Must be Read in Their Context*

Words and phrases used in an Act must be read in their context. The main rule is that, words and phrases are to be construed in the sense in which they are ordinarily used, but where they have a technical meaning in law they must be construed in accordance with the meaning.[52]

4. *Departure from the Literal Construction of Statutory Language*

The main rule of construing taxing statute as discussed above, require that one should look simply at what is clearly said. However, courts may sometimes depart from literal construction where such construction leads to an absurd result which cannot have been contemplated. As observed in the case of **AG v. Hallet**[53] such literal construction can lead to unfair and highly inequitable results. But where the words are not ambiguous courts will be bound by the literal construction even though unreasonable.[54]

5. *Misconception of Existing Law*

Where a statutory provision is enacted on the basis of a misconception of existing law, the law remains as it was and does not share such misconception. Such misconception cannot change the law.[55]

6. *Provisions Dealing with Tax Machinery*

Provisions dealing with machinery of taxation are presumed not to impose a charge and cannot be construed to defeat a charge.[56]

---

[52] Read the case of **Turner vs. Follent** (1973) 48 TC 614 at 619, 622

[53] 2 H & N 368 at 375. See also **Coutts & Co. vs. IRC** *(supra)*

[54] See the statement of Lord Evershed in the case of **IRC vs. Hinchy** *(supra)*. Also see **Pearberg vs. Varty** (1972) 2 All ER 6 at 11.

[55] Refer the case of **Davies, Jenkins & Co.** (1968) AC 1097 at pp. 1110 & 1112.

[56] IRC

7. *Tax Acts as a Whole*

Tax Acts are considered as forming a single code. Therefore, meaning of a word in one Act may be ascertained from words used in the Tax Acts as a whole.[57]

8. *Two Statutes Dealing with Same Matter*

Where two statutes deal with the same matter one may be used to explain the other. However, case law is not unanimous on this rule.[58]

9. *Consolidating Statutes*

The interpretation of consolidating statute should not be made in reference to earlier Acts. It should be noted that the above rules do not operate in exclusivity. All other rules and aids used in interpreting other statutes apply as well to taxing statutes.

---

57 See the cases of **Peney General Investment Trust Ltd. vs. IRC** (1943) AC 486; **Grantside vs. IRC** (1968) AC 553 at 602; and **Martin vs. Lowry** 11 TC 297 at 315

58 See Tiley, Revenue Law (supra) p. 38 for a critique of this rule.

3

TAX EVASION AND TAX AVOIDANCE

DEFINITION

The terms "tax evasion" and "tax avoidance," do not easily yield to definition. The object of both pursuits is the reduction or elimination of tax liability. The major distinction between the two terms is illustrated by the different consequences imposed in the event of an unsuccessful attempt by the taxpayer. In the case of evasion the consequences are criminal in nature and lead to the imposition of a fine or incarceration or both. Avoidance of tax involves no criminal penalty, only payment of the tax plus interest since the tax avoided is considered as a debt due from the taxpayer to the government.

Tax Evasion

Tax evasion can simply be defined as the wilful attempt by a taxpayer to suppress or not to disclose income and, hence, not to pay tax thereon, where the law clearly stipulates the obligation to report the income and pay the tax. Ordinarily tax evasion involves:

1. Not filing an income return at all;
2. Filing an income tax return but wilfully omitting therefrom income earned by the taxpayer during the relevant year of income;

3. Filing an income tax return containing a wilful misrepresentation of the nature or amount of income earned;

4. Arranging for the receipt of income in a jurisdiction or form whereby that income will not come to the attention of the tax authorities. For example, receiving payment for services in cash which the taxpayer believes cannot be traced;

5. Characterising a transaction both in the books of account of the taxpayer and in the tax return in a manner so as to disguise the real object or benefit of the transaction. For example, recording an expense which has not been incurred in the income earning process.[59]

In other words, tax evasion involves the taxpayer failing to do what is required by law.

Case Law Examples

In the case of **Regina v. Branch**[60] the accused practised dentistry in calgary and admittedly had not filed tax returns for the years 1970 to 1973 inclusive. The issue was whether he had wilfully evaded payment of taxes. He pleaded that his omission to file returns for four consecutive years was not intentional, that he was emotionally washed up and thus could not attend to many of his affairs.

The court in finding the accused not guilty for lack of *mens rea* stated that:

> ... in my opinion the word evasion implies something of an underhanded or deceitful nature.... A deliberate attempt to escape the requirement of paying tax on income that had been earned. This intention can be inferred from acts of omission or commission. Certainly failure to file tax returns and to pay tax for four successive years might suggest an attempt to evade in some way the payment of taxes.

---

[59] This definition is also contained in cmd 9474 paragraph 1016.

[60] (1976) CTC 193

Owing to the evidence adduced before it the court found the accused to have harboured no intention to evade tax and so acquitted him.[61]

Tax Avoidance

Tax avoidance is generally taken to refer to those attempts by the taxpayer to eliminate or minimise their tax obligations either through openly arranging their income-earning affairs in a manner which takes advantage of the most beneficial provisions of the tax legislation, or to rely on reasonable differences in interpretation of provisions of that legislation. Usually, the taxpayer will enter into transactions which, while having legal consequences, have little or no real impact on their financial position.

Tax avoidance may be said to be the art of dodging tax without actually breaking the law. Lord Tomlin in **IRC v. Duke of Westminster**.[62] Observed that:

> Everyman is entitled if he can to order his affairs so that the tax attaching under the appropriate Acts is less than it otherwise would be. If he succeeds in ordering them so as to secure this result, then however unappreciative the Commissioners of Inland Revenue or his fellow taxpayers may be of his ingenuity he cannot be called to pay increased tax.

Therefore, tax avoidance is a transaction which:

a) Avoids tax;

b) Is entered into for the purpose of avoiding tax or adopts some artificial or unusual form for the same purpose;

---

[61] Other examples include the case of **Regina vs. Hummel** (1971) CTC 803 where the accused was charged with wilful evasion of the payment of taxes and making false and deceptive statements in tax returns. The court also acquitted the accused on finding that there was no *mens rea*. In **Regina vs. G.F.R. Hopper3** EATC 84 however, the accused was found guilty on the charge of omission of income from return, making use of fraud and giving incorrect information.

[62] *(Supra)*

c) is carried out lawfully; and

d) is not a transaction which the legislature has intended to encourage.

Note however, for a transaction to be treated as avoiding tax, three requirements must be satisfied.

First, the taxpayer must receive the amount which would have been liable to tax as part of his income but on which he avoids tax by some artifice or device.

Second, the avoidance of tax must be the end intended by the taxpayer in entering into the transaction which avoids tax. That is, the transaction has to be a deliberate act with a set purpose, one which would not be adopted if the tax saving element had not been present.

In **CIR v. Brebner**[63] it was held in accordance with the Act that where a person has obtained a tax advantage from certain defined transactions, the tax advantage would be cancelled unless the person who has obtained the advantage shows that the transaction or transactions were carried out either for *bona fide* commercial reasons or in the ordinary course of making or managing investments and that none of those transactions had as their main object or one of their main objects to enable a tax advantage to be obtained.

The facts of this case were that the appellant purchased a company in order to prevent its falling into rival hands who would have wound it up such as to cause prejudice to the appellant's commercial interests and other persons who had dealings with the company. After the purchase, the share capital was increased from capital and revenue reserves. Later capital was reduced and distributed to shareholders who used the money to pay of the loan for the purchase of the company to a bank.

It was held that here the requisite intention to solely obtain tax advantage was not proved. So much of the evidence indicated a *bona fide* commercial transaction.

But the facts of the case of **AR v. CIT**[64] satisfied the statutory test. The case involved a private company whose members were the

---

[63] 43 TC 705

[64] 2 EATC 202

appellant husband, his wife and children. After two years of operations the father transferred all personal assets and income to the company in return for a fixed annual income (annuity). In carrying out this transaction the appellant avoided and reduced his tax liability.

It was held that one of the main purposes of this transaction was the avoidance of tax liability. Note that the onus of proving that one of the main objects of the transaction was not the avoidance or reduction of liability to tax lies on the taxpayer as held in the case of **BD Co. v. CIT**.[65]

Third, the act or acts of avoidance must be systematic not exceptional.[66] For example, in the case of **Bisland v. CIR**[67] an assessee disposed of his shares in an attempt to avoid his tax liability on accumulated dividends. This was a single operation and exceptional. There had never been any other attempt of a similar nature or leading to the same result. The court ruled that the act of the taxpayer was exceptional not systematic and could not therefore be treated as avoidance to enable the Commissioner to make adjustments.

PRINCIPLE METHODS OF AVOIDING TAX[68]

1. **Income Splitting**

This entails the splitting of income between more than one taxpayer so as to reduce the marginal rate of tax chargeable thereon. For example, a wealthy individual may spread or fragment his income by forming a partnership restricted to family members thus avoiding progressive individual rates but the income of the partnership still comes to him as head of the family and the *de facto* owner of the firm.

For instance, in the case of **Millard v. FCT**[69] an agreement was made between a licensed bookmaker and a family company under which it

---

[64] 2 EATC 202

[65] 3 EATC 41

[66] Perhaps this is not good law or it is outdated. The word systematic implies a number of transactions of the same character.

[67] 20 TC 446

[68] Read 18 MLR 209 at 210 for greater detail.

[69] (1962) 108 CLR 336

was agreed that the company should take over and carry on the bookmaker's business and henceforth the bookmaker would carry on his activities as an agent for the company. The Commissioner assessed the bookmaker on the basis that sums paid by him into the company's account were included in his taxable income.

The court held that the profits made were derived wholly from the bookmaker's own activities, and the provision made by the agreement for the subsequent disposition of the profits was for the purpose of avoiding tax.

A similar decision was entered by the court in the case of **Peate v. FCT**[70] where a taxpayer who was a medical practitioner formed a family company which purchased his practice and equipment. He agreed to serve it for a salary.

In **Cecil v. FCT**[71] the device used to split income was the interposition of family company between the taxpayer's retail company and wholesalers or manufacturers. The taxpayer purchased goods from the interposed company, which itself purchased them from wholesalers and manufacturers, though the taxpayer could have purchased them directly at the same price. Using the interposed company the taxpayer managed to transfer profits from his retail company to the family company through the transfer pricing mechanism and hence achieving income splitting.

2. **Income or Asset Shifting**

This technique is achieved through the shifting of income or income producing asset to another person or entity in which the taxpayer has a beneficial interest and which is chargeable to less tax. Depending on the tax system, such person or entity could be a corporation, a trust, a charitable organisation, a firm, or any other entity which has preferential tax treatment.

For example, in **AD v. CIT**[72] Mr. A.G.S. created a trust to assist poor and needy muslims. He appointed himself and his two sons trustees. According to the trust deed the trustees had total control of the

---

[70] (1966) 40 ALJR 155

[71] (1964) 111 CLR 430. Read also **BW vs. CIT** 4 EATC 225

[72] 2 EATC 89

trust, conducted the business of the trust and provided all the revenue and property of the trust. Although the set up had all the hallmarks of avoiding tax, the commissioner failed in an attempt to assess the trustees on the profits made by the trust. The court held that only the trust was assessable to tax.

Also in the case of **AG v. CIT**[73] the taxpayer used a trust he had created to accumulate income and the court held that the same is not assessable in the hands of the trustee.

3. **Deferment of Tax Liability**

Taxpayers sometimes use devices such as issuing loans or in dealing with assets, dispose of them by way of non-taxable dispositions, to effect deferral until sometime in future, the payment of tax on income currently being earned.

4. **Sheltering of Income**

The sheltering technique entails the use of brilliantly hatched schemes because of the increased capabilities of the tax authorities to neutralise such schemes. Examples of the common schemes used to shelter income include the use of "tax havens" i.e. countries which are "low-tax" or which levy no tax at all; Or the use of shelters implicit in the domestic tax scheme such as the generous capital cost allowances, investment allowance, liberal deductions offered to agricultural and mining businesses. Sometimes the taxpayer himself may physically emigrate to another tax jurisdiction where tax incidence is low or may transfer his property to foreign trustees or to a foreign holding company.

5. **Capitalisation of Income**

Capitalisation of income means the conversion of otherwise taxable income into capital which may remain untaxed or taxed at a lesser rate; or into some form of intangible benefit to the recipient, the receipt of which will be untaxed; or into some form of income otherwise exempt from tax by the provision of the Act. For instance a taxpayer may

[73] 2 EACT 43

arrange for his income to come to him as a capital receipt in the following ways:

a) Letting property on lease at a large premium and a much reduced rent.

b) Selling securities before dividend is distributed and repurchasing them afterwords.[74]

c) Non-declaration of dividends despite large profits made and profits ploughed back into the company as capital. This technique is called the "transformer or levelling device."[75]

6. **Conversion of Capital Expenditure into Current Expenses**

Sometimes taxpayers may arrange for ordinary expenditure to be made in a form which qualifies as a deduction. For example, arrangement by a director or the company to own and run his car hence making motor vehicle expenses be expenditure exclusively incurred for the production of income, or an arrangement by the company to allow the director to go on business trip with family which in fact is a vacation.

7. **Dividend Stripping**

For example, a solvent company is bought by a shareholding Co., then a large dividend is declared and shares sold at a less than market value (loss) to the former shareholders which then is used as a basis for tax refund claim.

The case of **BD Co. Ltd v. CIT**[76] is very illustrative of the use of such stripping device. In this case, the appellant company which was in receivership at the instance of a debenture holder, owned half the shares in W. Ltd. which later company was in a position to declare a large dividend. If the dividend were declared the appellant company would be able to pay off the debenture holder and as a result the receivership would be terminated.

---

[4] See Newton's Case (1958) AC 450

[75] Read Hancock's Case (1961) 108 CLR 258; and Mayfield's Case (1961) 108 CLR 303

[76] *Supra*

The remaining half of the shares in W. Ltd. were held by L.W., who because of the income tax liability which he would incur if the dividend were declared was not prepared to agree to the declaration of a dividend. The receivers of the appellant company entered into a dividend stripping agreement with L.W., by which L.W., sold his shares to the appellant company for a certain (high) amount. The dividend was declared and the appellant company resold the shares to L.W., for an amount considerably less than the purchase price. As a result L.W. was enabled to realise a capital gain on which he paid no tax, and the appellant company received the dividends and as it had a loss for income tax purposes in excess of the amount of dividends declared became entitled to refund of tax paid by it on the profits out of which the dividend was declared.

The court, however, nullified the transaction holding that one of the main purposes of the transaction was the avoidance or reduction of liability to tax. Therefore, the adjustments order by the Commissioner was held to be appropriate to counteract the reduction of tax liability.

8. **Other Methods**

a) Valuation techniques designed to offer maximum advantage to the taxpayer;

b) The passing on of property with accrued capital gain or losses by one taxpayer to another so that tax consequences arise only when the other taxpayer disposes of the property in a chargeable transaction;

c) The structuring of a commercial transaction in a manner designed to produce the least tax burden possible by appropriate choice of alternative methods of concluding the transaction;

d) The purchase of an insolvent company which has made heavy loss so as to use the loss against future profits, or the forming of an estate at a loss while it is steadily improved so that it ultimately it sells for a nice capital profit;

e) Taking a new partner or retiring an old one so that the partnership can claim cessation of business whenever it suits it;

g) Arrangements between employer and employee which prejudice the Income Tax Department. For example, by changing the form of certain payment so as to put it outside the tax orbit. For example, treating part-time payment as honoraria.

MECHANISMS DEVELOPED TO LIMIT TAX AVOIDANCE

The traditional common law approach is based on the principle that fiscal statutes must be construed strictly.[77] The House of Lords in the case of **IRC v. Duke of Westminster**[78] laid down the doctrine that courts are prevented from going behind the legal effect of a transaction and taxing it as if the transaction had some different legal effect.[79] According to this judicial approach the Revenue Department carried the burden of showing that the taxpayer fairly fell within the scope of the charge.

In effect, as demonstrated in the case of **Ayrshire Pullman Motor Services v. IRC**[80] the judges saw nothing inherently evil in tax avoidance as distinct from tax evasion.

In recent times however, "strict construction" of taxing statutes has come under attack by a trend which favours a more liberal construction aimed at giving effect to the intention of the legislature especially when interpreting anti-avoidance provisions because it is impossible for the legislature to foresee and forestall ingenious taxpayer schemes of avoiding tax.

Let us take an example of what transpired in **Greenberg v. IRC**[81] to demonstrate the ingenuity of taxpayers. The taxpayer wished to escape from paying tax on the profits of his company for say five

---

[77] Refer **Partingtom vs. AG** (1869) LR 4 HL 100; and 21 Law Times 370

[78] *(Supra)*

[79] *Ibid.* See, in particular the statement of Lord Tomlin at p. 763.

[80] (1929) 14 TC 754. Read Lord Clyde's observation at p. 763

[81] 47 TC 240

years. The company is a trading company. He causes his company to create a novel kind of shares, say 100 of them which were to receive all dividends declared by his company for the next 5 years and thereafter to receive only an ordinary preference dividend.

Suppose he expects his company to declare dividends of T.Shs. 200,000/= during that period; he sells these shares to a finance company for T.Shs. 200,100/= to be paid in instalments which are in fact dividends received by the finance company from his company. In this way he receives his company's dividends as capital, that is, in the form of the price of shares he has sold to the finance company.

The finance company here is participating in a scheme for tax avoidance. It will also benefit by treating the difference between the price which it paid for these strange shares and the nominal value of the shares at the end of the 5 years as trading loss and diminish the amount of tax it has to pay. That is, it paid T.Shs. 200,100/= for the shares at the end of the 5 years and by that time the shares are worth only T.Shs. 100/=. Therefore, the finance company could claim that it has suffered a trading loss to the true of T.Shs. 200,000/=.

A number of techniques have been used by the courts to put limits on the ingenuity of taxpayers in arranging their affairs so as to minimise tax. The **Duke of Westminster Case** (supra) has been reconsidered to a great extent. Now it is possible for the courts to render transactions or documents ineffective and hence counteract their intended tax impact; or transactions that are shown are taxed according to their real transaction where the same is discovered.

Criteria Commonly Used to Determine Tax Avoidance

1. *The Arm's Length Concept*

It is an underlying assumption of income tax law that profits or gains made by a taxpayer are achieved through the interplay of market forces which are independent of the taxpayer's control. This assumption often break down where parties to a transaction do not have opposing economic interests, but have, by virtue of the particular relationship between them, a common economic interest which enables them to arrange the terms of the transaction to produce the least amount of tax. Persons in such circumstances are said not to deal with each other "at arm's length" and transactions between them are referred to as "transactions not at arm's length." For example, related persons such as individuals related to each other by blood relationship, marriage or adoption or a corporation and a person or a related group that controls the corporation, and corporations which are subject to common control.[82]

2. *Inadequate Consideration, Reasonableness and Allocations*

Ordinarily consideration received in certain non-arm's length transactions is deemed to be Fair Market Value (FMV) for the purpose of determining the taxpayer's income. However, complications arise in cases of dispositions between spouses. Section 46(1) of the Income Tax Act, 1973 only covers employment income of a wife employed in her husband's business. It is unclear what would be the position in Tanzania where the spouses trade independently and purport to transact with each other.

As regards expenses, sometimes the tax authorities may limit deduction of expenses to only reasonable amounts. For example, where a businessman claims a deduction of entertainment expenses or expenses of running a motor vehicle used by a director in the course of his employment, and more often, the test of reasonableness is invoked to prevent closely held companies from avoiding corporation tax by means of large salaries, fees or commission to major shareholders.[83]

3. *Benefits*

At a very simple level everyone thinks of receipt of money as a necessary prerequisite to liability for income tax. There are, however, many substantial benefits that an individual may receive which increase his or her economic wealth but do not come directly in the form of money. Section 5(2)(b) of the Income Tax Act, 1973 brings such benefits within the scope of tax. But, even where the benefit is conferred on a non-employee for example, where a company confers a benefit on its shareholder such a benefit could be taxed.

---

[82] Read the cases of **Dunkelman vs. MNR** (1959) CTC 375; and **Wertman vs. MNR** (1964) CTC 252.

[83] See **CIT vs. P. Co. Ltd.** 1 EATC 131

Consider the case of **MNR v. Pillsbury Holdings Limited**[84] Pillsbury borrowed money from two subsidiaries to buy shares in them i.e. it bought the subsidiaries with the subsidiaries' money. Interest on the loans, which was expressed to be payable was waived by the subsidiaries after a formal request to do so was received from Pillsbury. In the same request Pillsbury offered to pay back immediately the full amount of the loans, which repayment was accepted. Revenue Canada sought to tax the interest waived as a benefit to Pillsbury.

The defendant taxpayer in the above case successfully defended themselves because the Court found that the consideration offered by the defendant in exchange for cancellation of the interest i.e. immediate payment of a large amount of principal in consideration of interest being cancelled, did not smack of a tax avoidance scheme. The court apparently would have held in favour of Revenue Canada if the circumstances of the case were suspicious.

4. *Employees*

There is a tendency which has recently gained momentum particularly with high salaried employees to attempt, in the name of tax planning, to replace salary income with some form of untaxed "fringe benefit" or into income, the tax on which will be deferred. Examples of most common fringe benefits include stock options, company cars, pension plan contributions, free housing and a horde more.

5. *The Business Purpose Test*

This test rests on the judicial principle that substance and not form should determine the results of a transaction. Various judicial doctrines have been invoked to impugn dealings which would otherwise effect a reduced tax. The concept of a "sham" which is used to strike down acts done or documents executed that purposely give the appearance of legal rights and obligations between parties which differ from the actual legal relations that are intended to be created; or "step transactions" where tax consequences are determined by the ultimate result of a series of transactions without regard to separate intervening steps; or "incomplete transactions" where a court can, for income tax purposes, disregard a

---

[84] (1964) CTC 294

transaction because all the necessary legal steps to implement it were not followed; and the "business purpose test" under which binding legal rights and obligations created by the taxpayer will be ignored if there was no business purpose to the transactions and the sole purpose for them was to minimise income tax payable.[85]

Statutory Mechanisms for Preventing Avoidance and Evasion

The Income Tax Act, 1973 contains several provisions which have been enacted with a view to the curbing of tax avoidance and evasion. A survey of these scattered provisions in the Act may be of great assistance to a student of taxation law.

Section 27 empowers the Commissioner of Income Tax to make adjustments which may lead to charging of higher amounts of tax to counteract the avoidance (or evasion) transaction thus making such transactions void for tax purposes.

Section 28 empowers the Commissioner to deem dividends declared and levy a tax where a private company defaults to declare a dividend.[86]

Sections 29, 30 and 54 are aimed at preventing the use of trusts as *conduit pipes* or devices for accumulating capital.

Section 33(5) aims at neutralising the device of changing accounting periods in order to take advantage of changes in tax rates during a year of income thereby reducing tax.

Section 46(1) counteracts the income splitting device between husband and wife.

Sections 57 and 58 imposes obligations on taxpayers to file returns of income and declare their chargeability to tax.

Sections 79 and 80 deals with taxpayers who attempt to avoid or evade tax by defaulting to file income returns or by submitting unreliable

---

[85] See the case of **Stubart Investments Ltd vs. The Queen** (1984) CTC 294

[86] However, this section should be read subject to the restrictions contained in the *Finance Act 1980* and formerly, reference had to be made to the *Companies (Regulation of Dividend, Surpluses and Miscellaneous Provisions) Act, 1972* Act No. 22 of 1972. This Act has been repealed in a manner which did not consider good tax administration. It has almost paralyzed the applicability and effectiveness of section 28. The repeal was unreasonable because the few offending provisions of the Act, and which irritated the business community could simply be excised from the Act and leave other useful provisions intact.

or fraudulent returns. These sections empower the commissioner to raise estimated assessments.

Section 74 empowers the Commissioner to examine books of account or records held by any person.

Sections 63 to 73 empower the Commissioner to require returns from specified taxpayers who would not ordinarily be required to submit returns.

Section 106 aims at enforcing tax payment by requiring any persons wanting to leave the country to obtain a tax clearance certificate.[87]

Section 114 to 125 prescribe offences and stiff penalties for specified breaches of the Act.

[87] This provision is now repeal, though under strange dictates. However, it is argued that the said provision was raising human rights concerns regarding the constitutional right of freedom of movement.

4

GENERAL SCHEME OF INCOME TAXATION IN TANZANIA

INTRODUCTION

A fundamental question with respect to any legal rule is, *who is subject to its application.* This is crucial in considering the application of a tax statute. There are two basic questions to ask in relation to the basis of taxation. First, which person or group of persons should be taxed; and second, which basis should be chosen for imposing taxation.

Alternative Bases for Taxation

The most common bases for imposing income tax used by nations are citizenship or nationality, domicile, residence, country of source and country of destination.

Citizenship or Nationality

This tax basis may be expressed in terms of the traditional obligation of every citizen or national to help support the state through taxation whether the citizen is living within or without the state's boundaries. It tends to emphasis (unduly) the political connection between a person and a country. Although taxation based on citizenship or nationality is an easy test to apply, it attaches an exaggerated and outdated importance to the jurisdiction in which an individual (or corporation) was born or obtained nationality. It could also lead to tax evasion by expectant parents awaiting the birth of their child in a tax haven.

Domicile

Domicile is often used as a basis for income taxation and inheritance or estate taxation with respect to death taxes. Domicile of choice involves two elements; one is the fact of presence within the jurisdiction; and two, the present intention on the part of the individual to maintain his permanent home in the jurisdiction. This basis frequently raises the problem of interpretation and is too rigid a basis for income taxation which must be levied perforce on an annual basis.

Country of Source and Country of Destination

Most taxing systems use a combination of citizenship, domicile and residence to levy tax and also use some concept of taxation by source. By this basis tax is imposed because income comes from the country of source through working, investing or carrying on business in such country.

For example, Tanzania imposes an income tax on persons who are employed in Tanzania, carry on business in the country or receive income from property in Tanzania even where they are not resident in Tanzania. On the other hand, Tanzania also imposes tax on the income earned by her residents who work in foreign countries, or carry on or receive income from investments in foreign countries.[88] Tanzania in this case is a country of destination of such income and treats the foreign income basically like domestic source income.

Residence

Residence is the main basis of income taxation in Tanzania. Under sub-section 3 (1) (a) of the Act, income of taxpayers who are resident in Tanzania which accrued worldwide is subject to taxation for that year of income.

---

[88] See sub-section 3 (1)(a). Tanzania imposes income tax on her residents in respect of income earned worldwide.

Non-residents are liable to income tax on their income which "accrued in" or was "derived from" sources situated in Tanzania.[89]

Residence has been defined in the Act at three levels:

Residence of Individuals

Residence of individuals is determined in relation to the year of income. Sub-section 2(2) gives two categories of individuals, namely, those having a permanent home in Tanzania and those having no permanent home in Tanzania.

Persons Having Permanent Home

Sub-section 2 (2) (a) (i) provides that if a person has a permanent home in Tanzania he or she will be a resident person for income tax purposes if during any part of the year of income in which he is sought to be taxed was present in Tanzania.

It should be noted, however, the terms "permanent home" bears no statutory meaning, therefore they should be construed in their ordinary meaning. That is, a place where a person resides continuously. Where he or she has a settled or usual abode. For income tax purposes if a person has a permanent home, say at Songea, but is currently living abroad, if in the course of the year of income he sets foot in Tanzania he is a resident.[90] It means, therefore, the lengthy of stay in the country is not a material consideration. It suffices to prove the fact of presence in the country during that year of income.

Persons Not Having Permanent Home

Sub-section 2 (2) (a) (ii) provides that if a person has no permanent home in Tanzania, he does not become a resident person merely by being

---

[89] Sub-section 2 (4) of the Act defines the meaning of the terms "accrued in" and "derived from" for the purposes of the Act. However, the meanings thereby assigned are only in addition to the ordinary meanings of the said terms.

[90] See also the difinition of "permanent establishment" under sub-section 2 (1)

present in Tanzania in any part of the year of income in question. He will be deemed to be a resident person for income tax purposes if:

i) He was present in Tanzania for a period or periods amounting in aggregate to 183 days or more.

For example, if X came to Tanzania for business purposes in 1992 and stayed from January 1st to April 30th, then left the country and returned on July 1st and left again on October 30th. In determining his residential status for the year of income 1992 the computation shall be as follows:

January 1st to April 30th - (30 dys x 4 months) =	120 dys
July 1st to October 30th - (30 dys x 4 months) =	120 dys
Aggregate number of days stayed in Tz. =	240 dys

Under sub-section 2 (2) (a) (ii) (A) he is a resident.

ii) He was present in Tanzania in that year of income and in each of the two preceding years of income for periods averaging more than 122 days in each such year of income.

Assume the year of income is 1995. X was in Tanzania in 1995 for 130 days. In 1994 he was in Tanzania for 150 days and in 1993 he sourjourned in Tanzania for 160 days. The computation shall be as follows:

Year of Income	*No. of days*
1995	130
1994	150
1993	160
Total no. of days in Tz.	440

Average no. of days in each year = 147 days.
Under sub-section 2 (2) (a) (ii) (B) he is a resident.

Note however, to be considered a resident under sub-section 2 (2) (a) (ii) (B) the average must be more than 122 days and not merely 122 days.[91]

---

[91] See the English position in the cases of **Levene vs. IRC** (1928) AC 217 (HL): and **IRC vs. Lysaght** (1928) AC 234

Residence of Corporations

Residence of a company or corporation is provided for under sub-section 2 (2) (b). A company or corporation will be deemed a resident if:

a) It was incorporated under a law of the United Republic;[92] or

b) If the management and control of its affairs were exercised in Tanzania during any period in that year of income.

As for the latter it has been a debatable question when to say that management and control of the affairs of the company is exercised at any particular place. Lord Loreburn in the famous case of **De Beers Consolidated Mines Ltd v. Howe**[93] remarked that:

> "... a company resides for purpose of income tax where its real business is carried on ... and the real business is carried on where central management and control actually abides."

Despite Lord Loreburn's observations it remained unclear as to where management and control of a company abide. In an attempt to resolve this crucial question Dixon, J. in the case of **Koitaki Para Rubber**

---

[92] Before the amendment effected by the Finance Act, 1998, Act No. 8 of 1998 the test was *"if the corporation was incorporated, established or registered under any Act or Ordinance or any law of Zanzibar."* Apparently, the amendment was not designed to achieve any improved administration of the Act. It appears it is one of those amendments prompted by the Tax Authority's reaction to a defeat. This amendment followed the decision in a case of *MacArthur and Baker International, Inc. vs. The Commissioner General of Tanzania Revenue Authority and the Commissioner for Income Tax* Misc. Civil Application No. 16 of 1996, High Court of Tanzania (Dar es Salaam Main Registry) (unreported) Whereby the court was called upon to determine whether by obtaining an approval under the Companies Ordinance, Cap. 212 enabling a foreign company to establish a place of business in Tanzania such a company qualified to be a resident person under the Act. The issue was whether the Certificate of Compliance issued by the Registrar of Companies denoted "registration" and hence the company is resident by virtue of being "registered under any Act". This case prompted a hurried proposal for amendment to be tabled before the National Assembly. Currently, far reaching negative consequences are unveiling.

[93] (1906)AC 455; Also in 5 TC 198 HL

Estates Ltd v. FCT[94] suggested that management and control of a company is exercised where its board of directors habitually meets for the purpose of conducting the business of the company.

However, this has been argued not to be universally true. That the critical question is to determine where the real business of the company is carried on, that is, not where it trades but rather where its operations are controlled and directed.

Recently it has been held that the question of residence is one of fact. In the case of **Unit Construction Company Ltd. v. Bullock**[95] the facts were that, the appellant company which was a wholly owned subsidiary of an English Company made certain payments to three companies registered in Kenya. The latter companies were also wholly owned companies of the said English Company. The appellants were entitled to deduct the payments if they were residents in the UK and carrying on trade wholly or partly in the UK. The court was faced with two issues in deciding the case.

The first issue was the applicability of Lord Loreburn's test in **De Beers Case** (*supra*). In the instant case it was difficult to identify any one country as the seat of central management and control which in the case was peripatelic (i.e. going about from place to place). The Court seemingly acknowledged that Dixon, J's judgement in the case of **Koitaki Para Rubber** (*supra)* gives solution to the problem.

The second issue concerned the decision of the House of Lords in the case of **Swedish Central Rly Co. Ltd. v. Thompson**[96] which laid down the proposition that although there was residence in Sweden by virtue of Central management and control being exercised there, there was also residence in England by virtue of incorporation there and the performance of administrative duties there.[97]

---

[94] (1940) 64 CLR 15

[95] (1959) Ch 147; (1958) 3 All ER 186; on appeal (1959) Ch 315; (1959) 1 All ER 591, CA; *revsd* (1960) AC 351; (1959) 3 All ER 831, HL

[96] (1925) AC 495

[97] This decision is considered an unfortunate one. Read also the case of **Sifneo vs. MNR** (1968) 68 DTC 522 which tries to demarcate between management *de facto* and management *de jure*. More cases on residence include the cases of **Egyptian Delta Land & Investment Co. Ltd. vs. Todd** (1929) AC 1; **Ogilvia vs. Kitton 5 TC; and Zehnder & Co. vs. MNR** (1970) CTC 85 which approved the Sifneo's decision.

Body of Persons Other Than Corporation

The test of residence for any other body of persons which is not a corporation such as a firm, trust, co-operative union, *ejusdem generis*, is similar to that applied to corporations which are not registered in Tanzania. Such body of persons will, under sub-section 2 (2) (c) be deemed a resident if management and control of such body of persons is exercised in Tanzania during any period in that year of income.

Minister's Declaration of Residence

Sub-section 2 (2) (d) empowers the Minister[98] to declare by notice in the Gazette that a person is a resident for the purposes of income taxation.[99]

IMPORTANCE OF DETERMINING RESIDENCE

The question of residence is of importance primarily because of the fact that by virtue of Sub-section 3 (1) the income subject to tax differs depending on the status of the taxpayer. In the case of a resident taxpayer it includes the gross income derived from all sources whether within or outside Tanzania which is not exempt income. Whereas, in the case of a non-resident taxpayer it includes only the gross income which accrued in, or derived from, Tanzania.

It is important to have the issue of residence of a taxpayer determined for various other reasons. First, personal reliefs are restricted to residents only. A non-resident cannot claim any of the reliefs offered under Part VIIIA of the Act.[100] Second, in determining income of a non-resident the law imposes certain restrictions in relation to deductibility of expenses.[101]

---

[98] As defined in sub-section 2 (1) of the Act.

[99] Formerly, one needed also to weigh the impact of sub-section 12 (1) of the repealed Companies (*Regulation of Dividends, Surpluses and Miscellaneous Provisions*) Act, 1972.

[100] Most of the reliefs under that Part were repealed by the Finance Act, 1998 (*supra*). These included, personal relief, married relief, and child relief. The reason given for the abolition of the reliefs was that the reliefs were insignificant and many taxpayers were not claiming them. A rather strange reason. The only relief remaining is in respect of insurance premium and contributions to approved retirement benefits schemes.

[101] For example, sub-section 19 (3) prohibits deduction of expenditure incurred outside Tanzania in ascertaining gains or profits of business of a non-resident person.

Third. Sub-section 42 (1) restricts the double taxation relief it offers to residents. Under certain circumstances even the rules for payment of tax as well as the applicable rates of tax are different when dealing with non-resident taxpayers.[102]

Persons Chargeable to Tax

The charge of tax is upon the person receiving or entitled to the income.[103] Section 3(1) charges to tax for every year of income, the income of:

a) A resident person which accrued worldwide; and

b) A non-resident person which "accrued in" or was "derived from" Tanzania.

However, there are other persons who may be charged to tax not because they received or were entitled to income as provided under Section 50, but in their representative capacity.[104] Sections 51 to 56 enumerates such persons. Section 51 provides for the assessment of the income of an incapacitated person. That such income shall be assessed on and the tax thereon charged on such person in the name of his trustee, guardian, committee or receiver appointed by a court.

The income of a non-resident person shall be assessed on, and the tax thereon charged, either on such a non resident person in his/her own name or in the name of his/her trustee, guardian or committee, or of any attorney, factor, agent, receiver or manager.[105] Section 52 lays down the rules for assessment and taxability of non-residents.

Deceased persons are provided for under section 53. The general rule is that the income which accrued to the deceased person or which such deceased person received before his or her demise, and which, if

---

[102] See sub-section 34 (1) and sub-section 33 (2) as read together with item 4 in the 3rd Schedule to the Act. See also the impact of sections 81 and 105.

[103] Section 50

[104] See the case of **Ransom vs. Higgs** (1974) 1 WLR 1594 at 1599

[105] Note the peculiar position of a ship master and an aircraft captain in subsection 52 (2)

death had not occurred, would have been assessed and charged to tax on him for any year of income shall be assessed on his executors or administrators who shall also bear the tax liability thereon.

Section 54 provides for the assessment of joint trustees. That is, where two or more persons are trustees assessment can be made on any one or more of them but each trustee shall be jointly and severally liable for the payment of any tax charged in the assessment.

Where a person has been assessed in a representative capacity in any of the above-mentioned instances the law imposes upon such person all the obligations and duties that would otherwise have been met by the person entitled to the income.[106] However, such a representative person is under Section 56 entitled to indemnification against all payments made by him in such representative capacity. The representative can effect such indemnification by retaining an appropriate portion of any money coming to his or her hands on behalf of such other person which is sufficient to pay tax.

The rule of assessment in a representative capacity has many case law examples. In **Applin v. White**[107] the taxpayer, an estate agent collected rents on behalf of clients.[108] He deposited money in his personal deposit account not marked "client's deposit a/c." He was assessed to tax on the interest. The Court held that the assessment was correct although the taxpayer was not beneficially entitled to the interest. He was the person who received it and therefore taxable.[109]

LIABILITY TO INCOME TAX

Income tax is levied or charged on an annual basis. The charge is upon the income which accrues to or derived by any person assessable to tax in the course of the year of income.[110] Therefore, in ascertaining the tax

[106] See section 55

[107] (1973) 2 All ER 637

[108] See also the cases of **Janet vs. CIT** (1964) EA 590; and **Karimjee vs. CIT** (1960) EA 521

[109] Note that, if the taxpayer had deposited the monies in an account marked as "clients' account" the ruling would have been different.

[110] Sub-section 3 (1)

liability of a taxpayer the tax authorities must compute the income of a taxpayer over a period of one calendar year.[111]

The Concept of Income

Sub-section 3 (2) enumerates sources from which income is chargeable to tax. It does not give an express definition of the term income. It only describes specified sources of income. There are literally various definitions of income depending on who is asked the question.

For example, economists, define "real income" as "a stream of economic goods acquired during a period of time", or "income" as literally "what comes in" first in money and then in what money buys.

Accountants usually talk in terms of "gross income" or "net income" or "gross profit" or "net profit". While one of their reasons for using these terms and assigning money amounts to them is to ascertain tax liability, they in the final analysis must rely upon what the law means by "income" in order to determine tax liability.

There is simply no all embracing or comprehensive definition of the term. Note that, it was not by accident that the drafters of the Act omitted or abstained from statutorily defining the term "income." Perhaps it was thought better to leave the doors of what constitutes income ajar for the purpose of netting more earnings in the income tax bag. Meaning of income is thus to be ascertained from ordinary use and general trading practices. But above all income is what the Act says is income or deemed to be income. The important issue for income tax purposes is not the definition of income but the distinction between income and capital because while income receipts are liable to income tax, capital receipts are not.

As pointed above, instead of defining income the Act classify income by reference to the respective sources from which it may be derived. Sub-section 3 (2) is a canvas provision. It charges to tax income from business, employment, annuities, salutary payments such as pensions, property, inheritances, alimony and other subsistence or maintenance allowances and deemed income i.e. what would not otherwise be called income but would be income because the Act chooses to call it income. For example, the payments listed under section 10 of the Act, balancing

---

[111] Sub-section 2 (1) defines a "year of income" to mean a calendar year.

charges under section 4 (d), and capital gains under the restored section 13.[112] All these are deemed under sub-section 3 (2) (e) to be income for income tax purposes.

Therefore, an amount received which does not derive from a source comprised or described by the Act is not chargeable as income. It should further be noted that in the Act the words used to describe income, for example, "gains or profits" imply that income is not only money actually received but may also include money worth, subject to the restriction contained in Section 3(3).

Distinction Between Income and Capital

What is taxable or chargeable to income tax is income and not capital receipts. As Lord MacNaughten observed in the case of **AG v. London Country Council**[113]

> Income tax if I may be pardoned for saying so, is a tax on income. It is not meant to be a tax on anything else.

According to Justice Pitney in the case of **Eisner v. Macomber**[114]

> Income denotes a gain derived from capital (property). It is not a gain accruing to capital, not a growth or increase in the value of the investment, but a gain, a profit, something of value proceeding from the property but severed from it. It is something that comes in or accrues. It is derived i.e. received or drawn by the recipient for his separate use, benefit and disposal.

Income is created. It is the result of application of efforts to capital by the taxpayer in the pursuit of gain. For instance, efforts such as labour or investment to create revenue. In short, the process of generating revenue. Therefore, receipts which accrue to the taxpayer from disposition of profit making apparatus or to agreements affecting it are capital receipts.

---

[112] Note that, the Finance Act, 1996, Act No. 13 of 1996 repealed section 13. The same has been restore by the Finance Act, 1999.

[113] (1907) 5 TC, 246

[114] (1919) 252 US 189

For example, a poultry owner, his capital assets will be the Chicken and gadgets. The proceeds realised from the sale of eggs are income. But if he sells the chicken (layers) the difference between the cost and proceeds constitute capital receipts and not income for purposes of taxation. The gain resulting from such a sale only represent an enhanced value of the capital asset at the time of its realisation. The rule is therefore that, where the owner of an investment chooses to sell it and obtains a greater price for it than he originally acquired, the enhanced value (profit) is not income.

CASE LAW ILLUSTRATIONS

In the case of **Greyhound Racing Association (Liverpool) Ltd. v. Cooper (Inspector Taxes)** [115] the appellants were a company which acquired a racing track and kept it for greyhound racing. The business later on failed and the debenture holders appointed a receiver who in order to realise the monies demanded by the debenture holders hired the track to another company which went into voluntary liquidation and paid a sum of £ 15,640 as full surrender value for the hiring agreement.

The issue was how to treat the surrender value. It was argued that the sum was a realisation of a capital asset and hence not income for taxation purposes.

The Court rejected this argument on the ground that the hiring agreement was a trading venture and not a capital asset.

Therefore, the principle is that where an owner of a investment chooses to sell or realise it and gets a greater value, then the enhanced value i.e. the profit he gets in not income for taxation purposes applied. In this case the appellant's receiver did not realise the capital asset i.e. the racing track. He hired it and therefore engaged in a trading transaction and therefore the amount he received on the hiring agreement was a trading receipt and not a realisation of a capital asset.

In **Y Co. v. CIT**[116] a partnership bought land for business. It was later dissolved and the land transferred to a new company. The Company was

---

[115] 20 TC, 273

[116] (1995) 2 EATC at 50

also liquidated and sold its investments. But before selling the land, it subdivided it into small plots thus selling it at a substantial profit.

The issue was whether the profits realised constituted income. The commissioner argued that by subdividing the land and selling it at a profit the company had engaged in business.

Court held that since the selling was of a capital asset the receipts though enhanced (i.e. profits) were capital receipts and not income.

In **Higgs v. Olivier**[117] an actor covenanted after finishing the making of one film not to act or perform in any film by any other company for a year and a half and in consideration thereto he received £ 15,000 which the commissioner sought to tax. He argued that the sum was not income but a capital receipt.

Court held that the payment was for a restriction extending to a substantial portion of his professional activities, that is, the payment was for interfering with his ability to perform which is a capital asset, and hence he was in receipt of a capital receipt and not income.

Note however, there are other payments which are compensationery. For example, payments for loss of profits, damages for breach of contract, *ejusdem generis*. These are income and not capital receipts since they are merely compensations which come to fill the hole.

For example, in the **Greyhound's Case** (*supra*) the payment was in respect of future profits which the receiver would have received and not a realisation of a capital asset i.e. licence to use as argued by the taxpayer.

[117] (1951) Ch 899; (1952) 33 Tc 136; 31 ATC 8

5

INCOME FROM OFFICE AND EMPLOYMENT

INTRODUCTION

There are three basic questions that must be answered in the context of employment income. One, is, who is an employee? Two is, when are receipts included in employment income? And three is, what is included in employment income? Note that, only an individual can have income from an office or employment and that the year of income for an employee is always the calendar year.

The terms "employer" and "employee" are defined under Sub-section 2 (1) but quite inadequately. Further, the Act does not define the terms "employment," "Office" or "employed."

The question whether a person is employed or self-employed and whether the source of income is employment or business is very crucial in determining tax liability. There are several reasons:

a) **Withholding Tax**

An employer must withhold tax at source from employment income and the withheld tax is held in trust for the crown.[118] An employer who

[118] See subsection 36 (4)

fails to withhold tax as required by law under Sub-section 36 (4) is liable to the government as if the amount of tax uncollected was a debt due from him to the government and interest is payable thereon.

Unlike employed individuals, self-employed individuals are not taxed at source. They are only required to file returns of income, and pay their taxes according to a different procedure.

b) **Scope of Deductions**

The question whether a person is employed or self-employed often arises in connection with the deductibility of expenses. Whereas an employee is restricted, for purposes of determining employment income, to the narrowly circumscribed deductions in the proviso to sub-section 5 (2) (a), a self-employed person has a considerably wider scope under section 16 and the Second Schedule to the Act.

c) **Taxation Year**

Employment income is taxed on the basis of receipt in a calendar year and an employee does not have any choice in the matter.[119] In contrast, business income is taxed on the basis of a fiscal year selected by the self-employed person subject to the Commissioner's discretion under section 31(1).[120]

The process of characterisation of income, that is, as employment or business income provides a fertile area of litigation and the cases are usually decided on a mixture of law and fact. One commentator has described the problem as follows:

> "It is often very difficult to determine whether a person is an employee or not. The best expression of the problem is to attempt to ascertain whether

---

[119] See subsection 31 (1) (b) read with subsection 2 (1) of the Act.

[120] This distinction currently does not apply. Even for persons other than the individual, the year of income is now the calendar year. The only difference is that, the latter category of persons submit their returns of income within six months from the end of the year of income to which the returns relate. This does not apply to employees.

an amount received by an individual is under an express or implied contract of service which would count as remuneration to an employee or whether it is received under an express or implied contract for services and thus would represent a business or profession. The question depends on whether or not a man-servant relationship exists between payer and payee. That this is a question of fact which must be determined according to the evidence adduced in each case.

Test Used in the Characterisation of Income

There is no single test that is decisive to determine whether an individual is an employee or an independent contractor i.e. a self-employed. Several tests have been evolved by the courts.

The Control Test

Traditionally, in determining the existence of a master-servant relationship the courts have focused on a "control" test. One of the best statements of the criteria relating to a determination as to whether an individual is under a master-servant relationship is found in Halsbury's laws[121] where it is stated that:

> "A servant (employee) acts under the direct control and supervision of his master, and is bound to conform to all reasonable orders given him in the course of his work; an independent contractor, on the other hand, is entirely independent of any control or interference, and merely undertakes to produce a specified result, employing his own means to produce that result .... To distinguish between a contractor and a servant (employee), the test is whether or not the employer retains the power not only in directing what work is to be done, but also of controlling the manner of doing the work."

In assessing the nature and degree of control the courts have considered four aspects of control.

i) The power of selection of the servant;
ii) The payment of wages;

---

121 *Halsbury's Laws of England*, 4th Ed. Vol. 23 (London: Butterworths, 1978) pp. 272-5; paragraphs 390 to 392.

iii) Control over the method of work; and
iv) The master's right of suspension or dismissal.

The case of **Isaac v. MNR**[122] is very illustrative of the control test. The facts of this case were that, the appellant, a registered nurse, worked in a Canadian Forces Hospital. She was a civilian hired on a day to day basis subject to the availability of military nurses. Thus she was paid per diem rate, did not get paid unless she worked and could be dismissed within 24 hours notice. She received no benefits or holidays and had not signed any form of contract.

The appellant did not consider herself to be a staff nurse, but rather a self-employed private duty nurse. Accordingly she deducted certain expenses from income. Commissioner disallowed most of the deductions contending that she was an employee.

The court held that she was self-employed under the common law test formed in **Gould's Case.**[123] The degree of control which the hospital had over the manner in which she performed her regular duties as a nurse were not sufficient to establish the master and servant relationship.

The traditional control test in the increasingly complex business environment is of limited value. The shortcomings of the control test reveal themselves in circumstances where it is difficult, because of the nature of the work, to exercise any control over the manner in which the work is performed. In particular the courts have found the test to be too inflexible in determining the issue in respect of professionals and highly skilled tradesmen.[124]

For example, in the case of **Rosen v. The Queen**[125] the plaintiff had resigned as a full time professor at the University of Ottawa and joined the civil service. However, he gave lectures on part-time basis, on data processing in three institutions i.e. University of Ottawa,

---

[122] 70 DTC 1285

[123] (1951) 1 All ER 368

[124] See the case of **Performing Rights in Society Ltd. vs. Mitchell & Booker (Palais de Danse) Ltd.** (1924) 1 KB 762 at 767

[125] (1976) CTC 462

Algonquin College and Carleton University. He purported to deduct expenses he incurred in the course of gaining or producing income from lecturing contending that he was not an employee of either of the three institutions where he gave lectures, but rather he was an independent contractor engaged in the business of lecturing.

The issue was whether he was an employee of the schools where he taught or whether he was an independent contractor engaged in the business of lecturing at these schools.

The court held that the control test was of little value in cases involving a professional man or a man of some particular skill and experience. It cited Lord Parker, C.J. in **Morren v. Swinton and Pendlebury Borough Council**[126]; Somervell, L.J. in the case of **Cassidy v. Ministry of Health;**[127] and Denning, L.J. in the case of **Stevenson, Jordan & Harrison Ltd v. MacDonald & Evans.**[128]

The court pointed out that the work done by the plaintiff for the three schools was done as an integral part of the curriculi of the schools. Thus the business in which he was actively participating was the business of the schools not his own. His situation as a part-time teacher was essentially different from that of a guest speaker or lecturer but it was not for that matter essentially different from that of a full time professor. Therefore he was an employee engaged for the purpose of delivering lectures on a part-time basis and not an independent contractor.

The Integration Test

The court in **Rosen v. The Queen** (supra) appears to rely on an integration test. That is, it examines whether an individual is part and parcel of an organisation. Where an Organisation hires an individual and the work of that individual forms an integral part of the organisation's business, then the hired individual is an employee.

---

[126] (1965) 2 All ER 349 at 351

[127] (1951) 1, 574 (CA)

[128] (1952) 1TLR 101 (CA)

The Economic Reality Test

This test examines several economic factors and draws from them an inference as to the nature of the relationship. In particular, four dimensions have been advanced involving (1) control, (2) ownership of tools, (3) chance of profit and (4) risk of loss. Thus in cases where the taxpayer supplies no funds, takes no financial risks and has no liability, the courts have applied the economic reality test and held that the taxpayer is an employee.[129]

The Specific Result Test

The specific result test has been used to distinguish an employee from a self-employed independent contractor. An employer-employee relationship usually contemplates the employee putting his personal services at the disposal of his employer during a given period of time without reference to a specified result and, generally, envisages the accomplishment of works on an ongoing basis. On the other hand, where a party agrees that certain specified work will be done for the other, it may be inferred that an independent contractor relationship exists.[130] Note however, there is a tendency on the fact of the Courts not to treat professionals as employees.

Attempts to Circumvent the Characterisation of Employment Income

The basic policy question is why should a taxpayer who earns T.Shs. 10,000/= a year under a "contract of service" be treated differently from a taxpayer who earns T.Shs. 10,000/= a year under a "contract for services." The obvious advantage to independent contractors of being allowed to deduct business expenses has led to adjustments of business arrangements by taxpayers seeking to avoid falling under the "income from an office or employment" classification.

One method to cut an employer-employee relationship is to use a business rather than an employment contract. This may change the relationship from a contract of service to a contract for services.[131]

---

[129] See the case of **Hauser vs. MNR** 78 DTC 1532

[130] See the case of **Lafleur & Pohs vs. MNR** 84 DTC 1478

[131] See the distinction in the cases of **CIT vs. AY Ltd.** 2 EATC 414; and **Fall vs. Hitchen** (1973) 1 WLR 286

Some tax planners have attempted to change the relationship by interposing a corporation owned by the former employee. For example, in the case of **Sazio v. MNR**[132] a football coach persuaded his team to hire his personal corporation to provide coaching services.[133]

What is Included in Employment Income

Gains or Profits of Employment

Sub-section 5(2) enumerates what constitutes gains or profits of employment. These include any amount received in respect of employment or services rendered. It follows therefore, gains or profits from employment need not arise necessarily from the employer. They may be amounts from a third party, such as tips and gifts. A voluntary payment to the holder of an office or employment is a profit of employment if it accrues to the holder by virtue of his office or employment notwithstanding that there may not be any legal obligation to make the payment.

For example in the case of **Blackstone v. Cooper**[134] a gift was held to be an emolument of employment. The facts, briefly were that, there were insufficient parochial endowments thus the clergy was underpaid. The Bishop appealed to the congregation for Easter offerings. A sum was paid to the pastor from the contribution. The issue was whether the sum was taxable as an emolument of employment. The court held that it was taxable since it accrued to the holder by reason of his office.

The case of **Colvert v. Wainwright**[135] involved tips to a taxi driver. It was held that though the money was received from a third party after the services were completed it was still part of the continuing employment as taxi driver, and because there is a general custom of tipping taxi drivers, the remuneration is expected as incidental to the employment.

---

[132] (1969) 1 Ex. C.R. 373

[133] See the definition of "employment" in the case of **Edwards vs. Clinch** (1981) 3 WLR 707; and the definition of "office" in the case of **Davies vs. Braithwaite** (1931) 2 KB 628

[134] (1909)AC 104

[135] 27 TC 475

In **Wright v. Boyce**[136] Christmas gifts to huntsmen employed on a wage, for personal qualities were held to be taxable as profits of employment. The court pointed out that the gifts were expected as a result of a general custom and accrued to the holder by reason of his office.

It is important to note that, emoluments of employment need not necessarily arise from the employer, but, as pointed out in the case of **Laidler v. Perry**[137] when it does so arise the presumption is that it is a reward for services and therefore taxable.

The above presumption is, however, rebuttable in that not all payments from the employer are by virtue of employment. According to the case of **Hochstrasser v. Mayes**[138] the test is whether such payments are reward for services past, present or future. Therefore, payments which are personal are not taxable as emoluments of employment.[139]

For example, in the case of **Ball v. Johnson**[140] a bonus payment for passing professional examination was held to be a reward for personal success and not for services and therefore not taxable.

In the case of **Moore v. Griffith**[141] the court held that footballers' bonus or prizes for Excellency were not reward for services but testimonial payments for personal talent.

Testimonial payments are special gifts for personal qualities or talent attributable to an individual. These are not taxable as emoluments of employment.

It is also impor tant to note further that, generally payments made after a contract of employment has been terminated are not taxed as emoluments of employment.

For example, in the case of **Durga Daas Dawa v. CIT**[142] the taxpayer was a sole distributor for a certain company. Later the agency agreement

---

136 38 TC 1

137 (1966) AC 16

138 (1960) AC 376

139 See *British Tax Review* 272

140 47 TC 155

141 (1972) 3 All ER 399

142 (1963) EA 695

was terminated and he was given a personal gift of Shs. 100,000/= in four instalments for long, cordial and successful business relationship. The sum was held not to be taxable because the payment was made on termination of employment.

It appear if the same was paid during subsistence of the contract of employment it would have been taxable as a reward for services past, present or future. But sometimes certain payments made after termination of contract of employment may still be taxable as emoluments of employment.

In the case of **Cowan v. Seymour**[143] payment to a voluntary holder of an office made after the completion of services for work well done was taxable as benefits of employment.

Gifts, Gratuities, Prizes and Awards

In Tanzania, from the wording of sub-section 5(2)(a) it appears such amounts could be taxed as amounts received in respect of employment especially when they do not constitute testimonial payments.

In the case of **Laidler v. Perry** (*supra*) the appellants appealed against the Commissioner's decision to tax a gift of £ 10. It was the custom of the employer to make Christmas gifts of £ 10 to employees thanking them for past services and for maintenance of good relations with the staff.

Section 156 of the Income Tax Act, 1952 - schedule E provided that:

> Tax under this schedule shall be charged in respect of any office or employment therefrom....

And in the Second Schedule to the Finance Act, 1956 it is provided that:

> The expression 'emoluments' shall include all salaries, fees, wages, perquisites and profits whatsoever.

---

143 7 TC 372

The Commissioner contended that the £ 10 were in return for services rather than as gifts not constituting a reward for services. Court held that the gift of £ 10 was taxable because the intention was to thank them for services past and obtain beneficial results for the company in future.[144]

In ascertaining whether such payments are taxable courts often appear to look at the regularity of the payments. That is, whether they are regularly expected by the employee, and the intention of the employer in making the payments.[145]

Benefits

Recent years have witnessed a substantial increase in the variety and quantum of benefits and advantages other than salaries and wages, provided by employers for their personnel, both at the executive and other levels of employment. With regard to company executives, these benefits are probably the progeny of high tax rates, which make salary increases less attractive. They are given inducements ranging from pensions, death benefits, life insurance, medical coverage, liberal expense accounts and allowances, to more immediate allowances such as club facilities, use of company cars, boats and other property. Employees other than executives have enjoyed extras in the form of pension, group life and health insurance, free or subsidised meals and lodging, profit sharing, paid holidays, annual vacations, commodity discounts, recreation facilities and free or subsidised transport.

Traditionally under common law benefits were not taxed because they did not constitute income. The common law conception of income is that only money or something capable of being turned into money can constitute income for tax purposes. A mere benefit or advantage which may be of value to the person who enjoys it is not includible in his income. The leading authority for this proposition is the decision of the House of lords in the case of **Tennant v. Smith.**[146]

---

[144] Read carefully the facts in the case of **Wright vs. Boyce** (*supra*) which also is illustrative on this point.

[145] Read the case of **Moore vs. Griffith** (*supra*)

[146] (1892) AC 150; (1892) 3 TC 158 HL

However, overtime many tax jurisdictions have brought within ambits of income taxation most fringe benefits. The general rule is that benefits are taxable as emoluments of employment.

It is important to note that it is the benefit to the employee and not the cost to the employer that is taxable. Whether the cost is deductible or not is a different question and will depend on whether it is regarded as wholly and exclusively incurred in producing the income sought to be taxed.

In Tanzania, sub-section 5(2)(b) brings to the charge of tax the value of any benefit, advantage or facility of whatsoever nature. However, the said provision excludes from taxation any fringe benefit whose aggregate value is less than Shs. 1,000/=. It is not clear from the statutory formulation if that sum refers to the cumulative value of the transaction, facility or benefit over the year of income or the standing value of the benefit per each transaction conferring a benefit to an employee.[147]

ILLUSTRATIVE CASES

a) In the case of **Heaton v. Bell**[148] a car loan by the employer for the personal use of an employee repayable through a reduction of the payable wage was held taxable. The provision of interest-free or low-interest loans by employers is considered a taxable benefits to an employee who receives a loan by virtue of his office or employment (the benefit is the imputed interest on the low-interest loan). In Tanzania the taxability of such benefit depends on the Shs. 1,000/= rule contained in sub-section 5(2)(b).

b) In the case of **Nicol v. Austin**[149] domestic bills of employees paid by the employer were held to be taxable benefits in the hands of

---

[147] See also sub-section 5 (2) (f) which renders taxable the benefit in the form of employer's premium to insurance on the life of an employee, save to an approved pension fund. Further, note the provisions of sub-section 5 (4) which restricts the description of "gains or profits" of employment in sub-section 5 (2)

[148] (1970) AC 728

[149] (1925) 19 TC 531

the employees. In Tanzania the taxability of such a benefit is not automatic because of the very poor drafting of sub-section 5(2)(b).

c) In the case of **Hartland v. Digginess**[150] it was observed that where a salary is paid "free of tax" the tax liability paid by the employer i.e. the tax advantage is taxable as an emolument of employment. In Tanzania it is likely to be treated as a cash receipt under sub-section 5(2)(a) and thus taxable.[151]

Imputed Income

Generally imputed income is taxable. However, in Tanzania there is a special restriction under sub-section 3 (3) which exempts from income taxation imputed income from certain sources. In the case of imputed income from employment, for example, living accommodation rented at less than the market rental value is not necessarily an emolument of employment. In the UK. the difference between the market rental value and the rent paid by the employee is included in the income of the employee and taxed. In Tanzania such income:-

a) Is not includible where the monthly total income of the employee excluding the value of the premises does not exceed eight hundred shillings[152]

b) In case of a service tenancy the difference between the market rental value and the rent paid by the employee is not an emolument of employment where the rent is paid on the basis of a general scheme relating to rents chargeable to such category of employee.[153]

---

[150] (1926) 10 TC 247

[151] See also the Provisions providing for "tax on tax" in Tanzania.

[152] See proviso (i) to sub-section 5 (2) (e)

[153] See proviso (ii) to sub-section 5 (2) (e)

Compensation Payment for Loss of Office

The general rule under English law is that such payment is not taxable as an emolument of employment because it is in the nature of a capital payment for the loss of opportunity to earn income or for the abandonment of a right to income under a contract of service. However, the compensation will be taxable as emolument of employment where it represents profits which would have been earned by the employee save for the cancellation. Where the compensation is in the form of an *ex-gratia* payment (i.e. golden or silver handshake) it is not taxable because it is payment for the cessation of employment.[154]

In East Africa the position was modified by the East African Income Tax (Management) Act, 1958 which by sub-section 5 (2) (c) thereto, treated compensation upon termination of employment as gains or profits of employment. Tanzania has adopted the same position. Sub-section 5 (2) (c) of the Income Tax Act, 1973 reproduces in verbatim the provision of the above mentioned 1958 Act and treats such compensation as gains or profits of employment. However, there are two restrictions under sub-section 5 (2) (c) (i) and (iii)

i) Where the compensation exceeds the amount payable on an unexpired term such excess is not income of employment; and

ii) In the case of a contract for an unspecified term the gains shall not exceed three years remuneration.

Note that, there are some decisions made under the East African law which appear to uphold the English position. Notably are the decisions in the cases of **AB v. CIT**[155] and the **Durga Daas Dawa's Case** (*supra*).

---

[154] Read the cases of **Mercer vs. Pearson** (1976) 51 TC 213; and **Henley vs. Murray** 31 TC 351

[155] 2 EATC 70

6. Any balancing charge under part II of the Second Schedule to the Act.[156]

Treatment of Benefits Stolen From the Employer

Benefits stolen from the employer do not constitute income in the hands of the employee since he has no title. According to the decision in **Rose v. Humbles (Inspector of Taxes)**[157] the employee is held to hold such benefits in constructive trust for the employer.

Deduction of Expenses in Respect of Employment Income

An emolument must involve profit or personal advantage to the employee. Therefore, reimbursement allowances for expenditure incurred by the holder of an office in the course of employment is not taxable.[158]

The test for the deductibility of such expenses is whether the amount sought to be deducted was expended by the employee wholly and exclusively in the production of his income from the employment or services rendered.

Deduction of Tax From Emoluments

In Tanzania tax from employment income is deducted at source through the operation of the Pay As You Earn (PAYE) scheme. The guiding principles or the rules are contained in section 36 which must be read together with the Income Tax (Deduction of Tax From Emoluments) Regulations 1975.[159]

a) *The Duty to Deduct Tax*

The Act imposes a duty on every employer to deduct income tax from the pay of all his employees regardless of their number. This duty is

---

156 See sub-section 5 (2) (d). This provision is anomalous. Balancing charges or balancing deductions are concepts associated with recapture or *recoupment* of depreciation. As such, it does not apply to employment.

157 (1972) 1 All ER314 (CA)

158 See sub-section 5 (2) (a) proviso (i)

159 GN 46 of 1975 made under sub-section 40 (1) of the Act.

contained in section 36. An employer need not be told to do so. Under sub-section 36 (7) the deduction of tax shall be in respect of every emolument whether paid weekly, monthly; annually or other intervals.

The term "emoluments" as defined under Regulation 2 of the above mentioned Income Tax Regulations of 1975 means wages, salaries, allowances and other chargeable income of any employee accrued or derived from his employment.

b) *Procedure for Tax Remittance*

According to Regulation 5 at the end of every month an employer shall compile list of the names of each employee from whom tax is deducted and indicating the amount of tax deducted and submit the same to the Commissioner.

Sub-section 36 (1) read together with Regulation 6 imposes upon the employer the obligation that the employer shall within 7 days from the date of the deduction pay the amount of tax deducted to a National Bank of Commerce branch or a Bank of Tanzania branch or other appointed person. Failure to comply with the stipulated procedural requirements is sanctioned with a stiff penalty under sub-section 36 (4).[160]

Note that under sub-section 36 (2) the Commissioner has power to direct an employer to deduct from an employee's emolument not only tax due in respect of employment income but also tax due from such other chargeable income which the employee may have.

c) *Method Used to Compute Tax Payable*

Income tax, as observed earlier, is levied on an annual basis.[161] Therefore the first step in computing the tax payable on employment income is to ascertain the annual income of the employee. For example, the annual income of an employee earning T.Shs. 6,000/= a month x 12 months is T.Shs. 72,000/= per annum.

---

[160] See also Regulation 10

[161] Sub-section 3 (1)

Having ascertained the employee's annual income, the next step is to ascertain the employee's monthly income by dividing the annual income ascertained in the first step above over a period of twelve months i.e. T.Shs. 72,000/= - 12 months = T.Shs. 6,000/= per month.

The third step is to add to the sum of monthly income whatever benefits chargeable to tax. For example, an employee earning a monthly salary of T.Shs. 6,000/= during the year of income is housed by his employer for the whole year and he was charged T.Shs. 300/= per months as rent.

Monthly pay	Shs. 6,000.00/=
Add housing 15%[162] of Shs. 6,000/=	900.00/=
Less: rent charged ... 300/=	600.00/=
Total monthly income	6,600.00/=

The amount so ascertained is then subject to the rates in the Third Schedule (or the Tax Tables). For example, according to the 1986 rates T.Shs. 6,600/= was taxed at Shs. 1,400/= plus 40% of the amount in excess of Shs. 6,000/=.

Therefore $\frac{600 \times 40}{100}$ = 240.00/= + 1,400.00/= T.Shs. 1,640.00/=

The tax payable in the instant example is therefore T.Shs. 1,640/= if the taxpayer was not entitled to any personal relief under Part VIIIA of the Act. Where the taxpayer is entitled to any of the personal reliefs available, the amount of the relief is then deducted from the tax computed as hereabove.[163]

---

[162] Subsection 5 (2) (c) read together with subsection 5 (3)

[163] As noted earlier, personal reliefs are now restricted to insurance premium and contributions to approved pension schemes.

6

INCOME FROM PROPERTY AND BUSINESS

INCOME FROM PROPERTY

Sub-section 3 (2) (a) (iii) charges to tax gains or profits from any right granted to any other person for use or occupation of any property. Section 6 defines gains or profits from property to include royalty, rent, premium or like consideration received for the use or occupation of property. It should be noted that the Act is silent on whether or not the recipient of income from property must be the owner of the property which produces the income. For example, in the UK case of **Masson v. Innes**[164] a famous author who was about to publish a new book made a gift of his rights in the book to his father. The purpose was to augment his father`s small pension. What would be the tax implication of this transaction to the father? the author?

Or where a taxpayer who is the owner of a bond, retains the bond but gives away the right to receive the interest? Or where a subsidiary company claims income earned from property belonging to a parent company?

---

[164] (1967) 2 All ER 926

In Tanzania, the wording of sub-section 12 (1) appears to suggest that ownership of property is crucial in determining chargeability to tax of receipts from property. However, the provision is very restrictive, in that, it only deals with contracts of hiring. It could safely be said that in Tanzania the law in this respect is quite unclear. It appears that, only departmental practice may throw some light on the question whether income from property means that only the owner of the property can receive income from it.

Another problem in the taxation of income from property is the treatment of imputed income which distinguishes property income and property use. For example, a taxpayer who occupies his own home instead of deriving rental income from letting to a tenant enjoys imputed income to the extent of the rent forgone. Or a farmer who consumes his own produce instead of selling it and buying groceries with the proceeds enjoys imputed income.

In the UK the most significant case on the question of imputed income is **Sharkey v. Wernher**.[165] The taxpayer in this case raised horses for sale but also maintained a stable of race horses as a hobby. Five horses were transferred from the horse-breeding farm to the personal stable. The issue was, which amount should be ascribed as income to the farm account. Is it the cost of breeding or a Fair Market Value (FMV) which would recognise forgone profit as part of the income. The House of Lords decided in favour of the FMV.

This decision has caused furore in other tax jurisdictions like Canada where there is disagreement as to whether Canadian law should follow the case. In Tanzania the position is clear. Sub-section 3 (3) declares that such imputed income is not income for purposes of taxation.

SPECIFIC KINDS OF PROPERTY INCOME

Annuities[166]

According to **Floyd's Case**[167] an annuity is an annual sum payable for a term of years, for life or in perpetuity and constitutes income in

---

165 (1955) 36 TC 275

166 See section 35 and sub-section 11 (2) (b) of the Act.

167 (1858) 3 H&N 769

the hands of the recipient. For example, in the case of **Williamson v. Ough**[168] a testator by will bequeathed an annuity to his wife for life then directed the surplus income to be divided in equal shares between the wife and three daughters. He authorised trustees during the life of his wife to make advance payments out of the income or capital of the trust fund. If paid out of capital to be recouped at later date. It was held that a recipient of payments made under this power on account and in advance of income, even where payments may actually be made out of capital is chargeable to income tax.

Note however, not every annual payment is an annuity. The annual payments could be deferred payments of a principal or income the right to which has been purchased by an outlay of capital. Thus annual payments for a disposed capital are not annuities.

Likewise annual instalments of the purchase price for the transfer of land payable over a period of time are not taxable as annuities. For example, in the case of **Secretary of State For India v. Scobble**[169] the appellant purchased railway company share option to pay full value or a gross sum in the form of an annuity for a term of years subject to interest on the annual payments. It was held that since the purchase was of shares and capital of the railway company the annual payments were capital payments and thus not subject to income tax.

From the above case the question may arise as regards the position of the purchaser. That is, since the payments on the purchase of the asset has a capital element, should be purchaser be allowed a deduction of the same in computing his gains or profits?

Formerly the position under English law was that such capital payments were not deductible. But the position is now changed as was held in the case of **Egerton Wanburton v. Deputy Federal Commissioner of Taxation.**[170] In this case, a father agreed with two sons to sell land to them. Part of the consideration being that they should pay him an annuity of £ 1,200 during his lifetime. The sons paid £ 659

---

[168] (1936) AC 384

[169] (1903) AC 299

[170] (1934) 51 CLR 568

to the father (each paid £ 329 10 S.). The Commissioner assessed the father on the £ 659 and disallowed as deduction from assessable income the sums paid by each son. It was held that the sum of £ 659 was income of the father, not an instalment of a capital amount as such it was taxable. Each sum of the £ 329 10 S. was allowable deduction in the sons' assessments as representing money laid out for the production of assessable income.

Boyalties

These are taxable under section 6 read with sub-section 3 (2) (a) (iii) Royalties are payments based on production or use as per the definition in the case of **McCanley v. FCT**.[171] They include, for example, payments by grantees of patents operating under licence such as payments by publisher to an author.[172] Also they include payments to owner of land for allowing certain benefits to be used by an outsider, for example, mining royalties and royalties for cutting timber.

It should however be noted that to constitute a royalty, payments need not be periodical. For instance, in the case of **Constatines Co. v. King**[173] a lumpsum award for patent use of an invention was held to be a royalty and thus taxable.

Further, it is important to distinguish between annual payments for the right to use which may be capital and annual payments for actual use which constitute royalty income. The former is non-taxable.

For example, in the case of **IRC v. British Salmon Aero Engines**[174] an owner of aero engines patent granted an exclusive right to manufacture the same to a manufacturer. Consideration payable in part by lumpsum money paid in three instalments, the other part in annual royalties. It was held that the lumpsum was a capital sum and the royalties income.

---

[171] (1944) 69 CLR 235 at pp. 240-41. See also the statutory definition in sub-section 2 (1) of the Act.

[172] See the case of **CIR vs. Longman's Co**. 17 TC 272 where it was held that annual payments to an author and holder of copyright for publishing translated version are royalties and taxable.

[173] (1927) 43 TLR 727

[174] (1938) 2 KB 482

Interest

Interest is chargeable to tax under first under sub-section 3 (2) (b) and, second, under sub-section 3 (2) (e) as read together with section 10 (e). While the former relates to bank interest, the latter brings into the scope of charge any interest. According to **Riches v. Westminster Bank:**[175]

> The essence of interest is that it is a payment which becomes due because the creditor had not had his money at the due date. It may be regarded either as representing profit he might have made if he had had the use of the money or conversely the loss he suffered because he had not had that use.

The repaid principal is not income in the hands of the lender. It is only the interest which is income.[176] But, per **Lomax v. Peter Dixon**[177] it is stated that there can be no general rule that any sum which a lender receives over and above the amount which he lends ought to be treated as income. For instance, payment of a premium on repayment of the principal debt may be regarded as capital payment.

In the case of **Green v. Favourite Cinemas**[178] premium for a lease payable in instalments apart from the rent was held to be capital expenditure necessary for the acquisition of property. Dividing it does not vary its character.

Two things must be remembered as regards the taxability of interest income in Tanzania. First, sub-section 3 (2) (b) declares that interest income subject to tax is only the amount net of an exemption of the initial One Hundred Fifty Thousand shillings of any income accruing as interest on monies saved in any bank operating in Tanzania. Second, that payment of interest is an allowable expense under sub-section 16 (3) (a).

---

[175] (1947) AC 390 at 400; 15 TC 314

[176] Read (1926) AC 205 at 213.

[177] (1943) 1 KB 671 at 677; 25 TC 353

[178] 15 TC 390

Discounts

In other tax jurisdictions there have been problems regarding treatment of discounts. In the financial markets debt obligations are often sold at a discount partly because that is the easiest way of honing the effective interest rate.

For example, a company might put out an issue of 7 3/8%, 20 year debt obligations but only charge the purchaser Shs. 995/= per Shs. 1,000/= face amount of obligation. In effect the purchaser will receive the Shs. 5/= discount 20 years from the date of purchase.

The issue is whether the discount should be treated as interest and thus deductible under sub-section 16 (3) (a) and whether it should be treated as income in the hands of the recipient.

In the Canadian case of **Wood v. MNR**[179] the Supreme Court stated that a "discount" is not properly treated as "interest" although it may be income from a business if the facts so indicate. That if the discount cannot be treated as income from a business, it would presumably be treated as a capital gain to the recipient.

In Canada the **Income Tax Act** provides two alternatives in dealing with discounts. On one hand if a debt obligation is issued at a "deep discount" by a government body or other tax exempt issuer, then the deep discount shall be treated as income in the hands of the recipient, [180] and on the other hand if the issuer is a payer of taxes then he can deduct the discount as an expense so long as the discount is shallow.[181] In Tanzania the Act is silent on this issue and perhaps taxpayers are to simply look at departmental practice until such time a provision to provide for discounts is enacted or any such time that the judicial authorities make a pertinent ruling.

Dividends

Dividend is income from property. It accrues to the taxpayer as income on an investment. The charging provision for dividend is sub-section

---

[179] (1969) CTC 57

[180] See sub-sections 16 (2) & (3)of the Canadian Income Tax Act

[181] See sub-section 20 (1) (f) (i) of the Canadian Income Tax Act.

3 (2) (b) read together with section 7. The taxation of dividends shall be dealt with further under the topic on corporate distributions.

Rent, Commission and Other Income on Leases

These are governed by sections 3 (2) (a) (iii) read together with section 6. The general principle is that any consideration received on lease, whether it takes the form of periodical payments in the nature of rent or wholly by premium or payment in kind is taxable income.

In **Green v. Favourite Cinemas** (*supra*) it was held that rent payable on a lease for occupation of premises is income in the hands of the recipient.

In **AL v. CIT**[182] there was a lease for 10 years. Consideration was in the form of a premium plus monthly rental payable. It was held that the premium was taxable as revenue because it was received in respect of user of asset as distinct from realisation of asset. This means, premium payable on the price of an asset is not income but a capital payment. It is, however, important to distinguish two situations. Whether the source of income is property ownership or a rental business. In the latter the source of income will be business and thus taxable under sub-section 3 (2) (a) (i) while in the former the source of income will be property and therefore taxable under sub-section 3 (2) (a) (iii).

INCOME FROM BUSINESS

Sub-section 3 (2) (a) (i) read with section 4 charges to tax gains or profits from a business. The term "business" is defined under sub-section 2 (1) to mean any form of trade, profession or vocation. It does not include employment. By section 4, where a business is carried on or exercised partly within and partly outside Tanzania by a resident person, the whole of the gains or profits from such business are deemed to have accrued in or derived from Tanzania.

The Act apparently throws no light on what the terms "carrying on business" means, and the definition offered is inexhaustive and of little

---

[182] 2 EATC 148

help in ascertaining income from business.[183] For example, when do particular activities constitute trading? Would a person or an association if persons buying and selling land or securities speculatively be considered to be carrying on a business i.e. trading? Or the gains realised treated as capital gains?[184] Or would a professional who offers his services for hire to an institution be in receipt of employment income or be considered to be carrying on a business? Or would a person who deals in letting houses or rooms be in receipt of income from property (rent)? Or would he be in receipt of business income?

It is very important to make the distinctions clear. Taxpayers would normally prefer to be categorised as being in receipt of business income because of the much greater scope for deductions for expenses incurred in respect to income from a business. As observed by Forbes, J. in the case of **The Trustees of A.D. Charitable Business Trust v. CIT.**[185]

> The dividing line between what does and what does not amount to the carrying on of business is not always easy to ascertain.

Therefore, whether particular activities constitute trading is a question of fact to be ascertained from the general and ordinary understanding of the word. Usual practice of traders will also help to ascertain whether trade is being carried on. It should be noted however, compliance with trading laws is not a material point in determining whether trade is carried on. For example, even criminal activities like trading without a valid licence, or operating an unregistered company would still be trading and profits liable to income tax.[186] This principle raises some

---

[183] Even after considering the extended meaning contained in the definition of the term "trade" under sub-section 2 (1)

[184] See the case of **California Copper Syndicate vs. Harris** 5 TC 165

[185] 2 EATC 89

[186] Read the following illustrative cases on this point. **Mann vs. Nash** (1923) 16 TC 523 where illegal trading income was held to be taxable; **Lindsay vs. IRC** 18 TC 43 where profits of selling stolen goods were held not taxable on the principle that the vendor had no title to the goods; and **Southern vs. AB** 18 TC 59 – illegal trading taxable.

public policy questions such as, should the state share in the profits of crime? Will profits of prostitution be taxable? If so, should the state share in the spoils of immoral activities?[187]

Meaning of "Gains or Profits"

The fundamental rule in taxing income from business is that a distinction must be drawn between gains of an income and those of a capital nature. As pointed out by Lord Greene, M.R. in the case of **Henriksen v. Grafton Hotel Ltd**[188].

> It frequently happens in income tax cases that the same result in a business sense can be secured by two different legal transactions, one of which may attract tax and the other not.

A common example is gains arising from the disposition of property. These may constitute income where such dispositions arise in the course of business, and may not where they arise other than in the course of business.[189] Many other amounts may be treated as income or capital depending on the circumstances. For example, premiums for the granting of leases, discounts or premiums on loans, amounts received as a result of the breach or cancellation of a contract, proceeds of insurance (apart from life insurance), foreign exchange profits, payments of damages, government subsidy payments and the proceeds of expropriation of property.

In many cases difficulties have arisen in determining whether particular gains, in the circumstances of particular cases, are properly regarded as being of an income or of a capital nature. Courts have developed several tests commonly referred to as "badges of trade" in distinguishing ordinary income and capital gains.[190]

---

[187] More cases on this topic include the cases of **Graham vs. Green (Inspector of Taxes)** (1925) 2 KB 37; 9TC 309; **The A.E. Investment Trust Ltd. vs. CIT** 2 EATC 99; and **Ryall (Inspector of Taxes) vs. Hoare & Honeywill** (1923) 2 KB 447.

[188] (1942) 1 A.E.R. 678 at 682

[189] See the case of **Executors of the Estate of Sheikh Fazal vs. CIT** 4 EATC 158

[190] See the case of **R vs. CIT** 1 EATC 172

Badges of Trade[191]

The Subject Matter of the Realisation

While almost any form of property can be acquired to be dealt in, those forms of property, such as commodities or manufactured articles which are normally the subject of trading are only very exceptionally the subject of investment. Also property which does not yield to its owner an income or personal enjoyment merely by virtue of its ownership is more likely to have been acquired with the object of a deal than property does. In the case of **Grainger & Sons v. Gough**[192] Lord Davey observed that:

> Trade in its largest sense is the business of selling, with a view to profit, goods which the trader has either manufactured or himself purchased.

The Length of the Period of Ownership

Generally, property meant to be dealt in is realised within a short time after acquisition.[193]

The Frequency or Number of Similar Transactions by the Same Person

If the realisations of the same sort of property occur in succession over a period of years or there are several such realisations at about the same date a presumption arises that there has been dealing in respect of each.

The rationale for such presumption is based on the experience that trading activities will normally involve repetitive or successive activities of the same or similar kind. It was observed in the case of **H. Co v. CIT**[194] that trading implies some continuity and repeated acts of buying and selling in same or other lines of business.

---

[191] Cmd. 9474 paragraph 116

[192] (1896) 3 RTC 462 at 474; See also the cases of **IRC vs. Fraser** 24 TC 498 at 502-3; and **California Copper Syndicate vs. Harris** (*supra*)

[193] See the court's reasoning in the case of **Turner vs. Lust** 42 TC 517 at 522-3

[194] 1 EATC 65

However, frequency of similar transactions is simply a presumption of trading. So even where there is only a single transaction i.e. "an isolated transaction" one may still be trading.

For example, in the case of **Pickford v. Quick**[195] the appellant was involved in four isolated transactions which netted him a big profit. Taken separately each transaction could be said to be of a capital nature, but when examined together they formed a pattern of trading. The court held that the profits were taxable as profits of business.

In the ease of **Martin v. Lowry**[196] the appellant was a merchant of agro-machinery. He purchased a large quantity of linen intending to resale at profit. He sold the linen piecemeal over a period of seven months. The court held that the purchase and resale was trading.

The doctrine of "isolated transaction" has been very well explored by the courts. In East Africa the case of **CIT v. Sydney Tate**[197] is an important case to students of taxation law because it reviews most of the important decisions on this subject.[198]

Supplementary Work on or in Connection With the Property Realised

If the property is worked up in any way during the ownership so as to bring it into a more marketable condition; or if any special exertions are made to find or attract purchasers, such as the opening of an office or large-scale advertising, there is some evidence of dealing. For when there is an organised effort to obtain profit there is a source of taxable income. But if nothing at all is done the suggestion tends the other way.

The case of **Cayzer v. CIR**[199] is the authority for the proposition that large development expenditure may be consistent with trading.

---

[195] (1927) 13 TC 251

[196] (1927) AC 312

[197] 3 EATC 417

[198] Other illustrative cases include the cases of **Trivedi vs. CIT** 2 EATC 177 where a practicing accountant was involved in selling property; **CIT vs. N.R. Bapoo** 2 EATC 397 which discusses the applicability of the doctrine of isolated transactions in East Africa; **CIR vs. Toll** 34 TC 14 at 19; **Cayzar Irringad Co. vs. CIR** 24 TC 491; and **Leach vs. Pogson** 40 TC 585.

[199] 24 TC 491

The Circumstances That Were Responsible for the Realisation

There may be some explanation, such as a sudden emergency or opportunity calling for ready money that negatives the idea that any plan of dealing prompted the original purchase. For example, in the case of **CIT v. Sydney Tate** (*supra*) the taxpayer had purchased a copper estate at £ 30,000 for capital investment which failed. It later subdivided it into some residential plots, effected improvements at £ 15,000 and engaged a real estate agent to make the sales who netted a huge profit.

It was argued that the taxpayer engaged in an organised effort to make profit hence trading. The court, however held in favour of the taxpayer on the ground that the initial intention was not resale of the estate, that the subsequent disposal by way of sell was forced by the turn of events and therefore it negatives the idea of trading.[200]

In the case of **Dunn Trust Ltd v. Williams**[201] there was a forced realisation i.e. sale of shares after death of the person. The suggestion that the original purchase was made with a view to resale is negatived.

However, where there is an element of speculation it may be evidence of trading. Such was the case in the case of **The Trustee of AD Charitable Business Trust v. CIT**.[202] A trust which was established for the purpose of carrying on some business purchased interests in four partnerships and later sold its interests in two firms at a profit, bought shares in two companies, sold its shares in one at profit, it further purchased underdeveloped property which was held briefly and then sold undeveloped.

The trust was assessed to income tax on the profits of these transactions because the court felt that the interests bought and sold were acquired in contemplation of realisation at profit when time was ripe.

---

[200] See a similar holding in the case of **Jones vs. Leeming** (1930) AC 415

[201] 31 TC 477 at 484

[202] 2 EATC 8

[203] 14 TC 490

[204] (1956) AC 14

In the case of **Rutledge v. IRC**[203] the speculative transaction involved the purchase of a large quantity (one million) of toilet tissue which were resold at profit. The court held that the profit was assessable to tax as trading income because the purchase transaction was effected in contemplation of a subsequent resale at profit.

Another example of a transaction entered into in anticipation of realisation of profit is the case of **Edwards v. Bairstone.**[204] In this case the appellants embarked on a joint venture to purchase a spinning plant and dispose of it at a profit. At no stage did they intend to use it as machinery or to hold it as an income producing asset. They approached potential purchasers and incurred various expenses in organised carrying out the venture and within two years sold the machinery in several lots at a profit.

Motive

There are cases in which the purpose of the transaction of purchase and sale is clearly discernible. Motive is relevant in such cases. If it can be inferred from surrounding circumstances in the absence of direct evidence of the seller's intentions and even, if necessary, in the face of his own evidence.

For example, in the case of **CIR v. Fraser**[205] the transaction was one of purchase and resale of whisky. The court observed that goods were purchased with a clear intention of reselling at a profit hence the transaction constituted trading and proceeds thereof income liable to income tax.

However, the profit motive is not a necessary requirement, it is only an indication of trading. Businessmen always contemplate a range of alternative possibilities in respect to the purchase of an asset, including the sale thereof if other considerations do not materialise.

In the case of **Griffith v. Harrison**[206] a merchant company having incurred losses changed its business to finance company. There was a single purchase of shares in another company. A dividend was

---

[205] 24 TC 498. See also the case of **Benyon vs. Ogg** 7 TC 125 involving a transaction of purchase and resale of railway wagons. It was held that there was clear intention to resale at a profit and therefore taxable.

[206] (1963) AC 1 at pp. 23 & 26

declared to which the finance company became entitled. Subsequently the shares were sold at a loss after the dividend was declared (dividend stripping operation). The purpose of the transaction was to enable the finance company to claim a deduction for setting off the loss on shares against the dividend to be received and thus lessen the tax burden.

It was held that the transaction had a character of trading and thus could not be negatived by the mere fact that it was entered into purely with the fiscal objective of obtaining deduction from the Revenue by the company as a taxpayer not as a trader.[207]

ASCERTAINMENT OF BUSINESS PROFITS

The usual starting point for the ascertainment of assessed profits of a business venture is the profit revealed by the commercial accounts and it is fairly well established law that ordinarily accepted accounting principles are acceptable in determining profits or losses for tax purposes except where the tax statutes require specific adjustments to those profits or losses.[208] Inevitably there are differences in interpretation in the application of accounting principles and there is therefore a wide body of applicable case law on this subject, particularly in the area of greatest contention, i.e. whether a given transaction is on revenue or capital account.

The Income Tax Act, 1973 deals very little with the receipts side of the account except to impliedly exclude profits from the sale of capital assets (other than interest in premises[209]) and to include certain receipts as deemed business receipts, such as compensation payments in connection with business activities. Whether or not the sale of an asset is an adventure in the nature of trade giving rise to a revenue profit or loss or whether it is an investment giving rise to a capital profit or loss is a contentious area on which there is a considerable amount of U.K. case law.

---

[207] See also the case of **IRC vs.ICL***R* 3 TC 105 at 113

[208] See **Usher's Wiltshire Brewery vs. Bruce** 6 TC 399

[209] Section 13

On the expenditure side the Act contains a number of regulating provisions for adjusting the commercial accounts as shall be discussed under various headings later. There are also a number of general principles on which there is a considerable amount of law and practice as shall be seen later.

DISTINCTION BETWEEN CAPITAL RECEIPTS AND REVENUE RECEIPTS

As most capital receipts and capital expenditure must be excluded from the commercial profit in arriving at the profit assessable to income tax, it is a matter of fundamental importance to be able to identify them. This is a very wide area of the law with probably more legal decisions related to this question than any other single tax question. Certain general principles can be drawn but in border line cases, there is no substitute for analysing the facts and researching the numerous decisions for parallel or similar circumstances.

On the income side the Act excludes only profits from the sale of capital assets, save for interest in premises under section 13, so in the circumstances where a receipt is of a capital nature but is not from the sale of an asset it seems there is no authority to exclude it if it arises from the trade, profession or vocation. This point has been considered by the Privy Council in the case of **CIR v. Far East Exchange**.[210]

On the expenses side, sub-section 17 (1) (b) disallows expenditure of a capital nature and it is only appropriate to consider here the general principles which govern the identification of capital expenditure.

One of the earliest tests was put forward by Lord Dunedin in the Case of **Vallambrosa Rubber Co. v. Farmer**[211] when he suggested that capital expenditure is that which is made "once and for all" whereas revenue expenditure will "recur year by year." Later on this test was expanded and qualified into what is now regarded as the classic and

---

[210] HKTC 1036

[211] 5 TC 529

[212] 10 TC 155

most often quoted rule, that of Lord Cave in the case of **British Insulated and Helsby Cables v. Atherton**[212] when he stated:

> But when an expenditure is made, not only once and for all but with a view to bringing into existence an asset or an advantage for the enduring benefit of a trade, I think that there is very good reason (in the absence of special circumstances leading to an opposite conclusion) for treating such an expenditure as property attributable, not to revenue, but to capital.

This rule must be treated with caution lest its wording be given too wide a meaning. It is perhaps relatively simple to identify the cases in which an asset is brought into existence whether it be a tangible or intangible asset. As regards the creation of an enduring advantage it is a failing of tax officials to refer to the **Atherton Case** and state that an expenditure in question gives rise to an advantage and is therefore of a capital nature. What must be remembered is that all expenditure gives rise to an advantage or it would not have been incurred. What is important is whether the advantage is enduring in nature and this implies something which is not necessarily permanent but of which the span is appreciably longer than that created by the normal revenue charge.

For example, an annual bonus to employees creates the advantage of willing service for a full year but if it is not paid next time, the advantage quickly fades whereas a payment to a departing employee in order to secure his covenant not to compete after he has left is a long lasting advantage and therefore of a capital nature.[213]

The fact that the intended advantage does not materialise or that the intended asset is not acquired and therefore expenditure laid out in anticipation is abortive is not however a ground for regarding it as revenue expenditure.[214]

A question may be asked as to what is the tax treatment of the cost of getting rid of some undesirable factor that is a hindrance to business. The Income Tax Act, 1973 does not cover this aspect expressly, however, according to the decision in the case of **Mallet v. Staveley Coal and Iron Co.**[215] the cost of removing an undesirable capital asset is of a capital

[213] See **Associated Portland Cement Manufacturers vs. IRC** 27 TC 103

[214] See **Southwell vs. Savill Bros** 4 TC 430

[215] 13 TC 772

nature because it creates an advantage as enduring as the asset itself. On the other hand, the cost of commuting a future onerous revenue charge is of revenue nature because it does nothing more than replace that revenue expenditure.[216] Similarly payment to terminate an onerous trading agreement is of a revenue nature.[217]

It should be noted however, although the cost of bringing into existence or improving or adding to an asset, together will all related incidental expenditure such as legal fees is of a capital nature, once in existence, the cost of protecting that asset is of a revenue nature.[218]

Compensation Payments in Connection with Business Activities

Where a payment is in the nature of compensation or damages it is necessary to consider to what it relates and it in fact normally follows the treatment of the transaction upon which the liability arose. For example, if it is damages arising out of a trading contract, say for the supply of faulty goods, it is of a revenue nature but if it is in respect of a capital asset, as in the case of a deposit paid for the acquisition of a ship and that the contract is not pursued, in fact a further sum is paid to secure the release of the obligation to buy the ship, it is of a capital nature.[219] The above rules can sometimes be modified depending on the facts of and circumstances of a particular case. Hereunder a survey is made of some variety of compensation payments.

a) *Compensation Paid Upon Compulsory Disposal or Requisitioning of Stock of Taxpayer*

Receipts from disposals of stock in trade are income. Disposal may be voluntary in the course of trade or by compulsory acquisition, for example, by government upon payment of compensation. Whatever profits resulting from such disposals are trading income.

For instance, in the case of **Newcastle Breweries v. IRC**[220] the appellants were brewers and wine and spirit merchants. They dealt in

---

216 See **Hancock vs. General Revisionary and Investment Co.** 7 TC 358

217 See **Anglo-Persian Oil Co. vs. Dale** 16 TC 253

218 See **Southern vs. Borax Consolidated** 23 TC 597

219 See **Countess Warwick Steamship Co. vs. Ogg** 8 TC 652

220 (1927) 43 TLR 476

rum, their practice being to buy raw rum and put it through a process and then selling the product. In 1918 a large stock of rum they had in Jamaica was requisitioned by the crown under the Defence Regulations for the use of the forces. The issue was whether profits resulting from the compulsory sale were assessable to tax.

It was held by the House of Lords that the compulsory acquisition of rum had the same effect as a sale in that it amounted to realisation of part of the stock in trade and therefore taxable.[221]

In Tanzania such proceeds would fall under section 4 (c) and be subjected to taxation as amounts received by way of damages or compensation for loss of profits.

b) ***Insurance Compensation for Loss of Trading Stock or Profits***

This is also treated as income from business under section 4 (c) and chargeable to tax. Note also that under sub-section 17 (2) (b) the taxpayer is not allowed a deduction of loss if the same is recoverable under any insurance, contract or indemnity.

In the case of **Glickstein and Son Ltd v. Green**[222] it was observed that where such compensation results in a profit the profit is assessable to tax.

The facts of the case were that, a quantity of timber belonging to a company carrying on business as timber merchants was destroyed by fire. The company kept the stock in trade insured against loss or damage by fire valued at replacement value. At the date of the fire the value of stock destroyed was very high owing to the boom and the insurance company paid at 477,838 in respect of the replacement value where the original cost was £ 160,824. The company brought into its accounts as trading receipts only the cost value and the balance of the insurance money was treated as a reserve fund.

It was held that the company must bring the whole of the money received as compensation into their profit and loss account as a trading

---

[221] See also the case of **FCT vs. Wade** 84 CLR 105; 12 TC 927

[222] (1929) AC 381 at 384

receipt in order to arrive at the company's profits for purposes of taxation. Per Lord Buckmaster:

> What has happened has been this, the timber which the appellants held has been converted into cash. It is quite true that it has converted into cash through the operation of the fire which is no part of their trade, but loss due to it is protected through the usual trade insurances and the timber has thus been realised. It is now represented by money, whereas formerly it was represented by wood. If this results in a gain as it has done, it appears to me to be an ordinary gain, a gain which has occurred in the course of their trade...

c) *Compensation for Breach or Rescission of Contract*

In the case of **Commissioner of Taxation v. Meeks**[223] the respondent, a smelting company contracted to sell a large quantity of concentrated ore to some purchasers to be delivered in instalments extending over a period of years. Under the contract the purchasers paid £ 63,000 in advance but before any concentrates were delivered the purchasers defaulted in further payments which had become due. Subsequently an agreement was made cancelling the original contract and entitling the selling company to retain for their use all the moneys paid thereunder. After deduction of commission and Brokerage the balance held by the company was £ 61,425.

It was held that the sum of £ 61,425 should be treated as profits from the smelting business carried on by the company and brought into account to ascertain taxable income of the company. It was stated that

> Damages received as compensation for non-performance of a business contract stand on the same footing as profits for the loss of which the damages are paid. Compensation is for loss of opportunity to earn that profit.[224]

---

[223] (1915) 19 CLR 568 at 580

[224] *Ibid.* But a question may arise, suppose the compensation includes exemplary or punitive damages, or compensation for emotional suffering awarded in lumpsum. Should the lumpsum be subject to tax as trading profits? Refer the case of **Southern Highlands Tobacco Union Ltd. vs. David McQueen** (1960) EA 490 (CA)

In the case of **Short Bros Ltd. v. CIR**[225] the appellant company contracted in February and March 1920 to build two steamers, but in November, 1920 agreed to the cancellation of the contract in consideration of the payment of the sum of £ 100,000 which was paid to it on 26th November, 1920.

The CIR included the sum as part of the trading income of the company for the year of income ending on 30th June, 1920 and levied a tax. The company contended that the sum was a capital receipt and therefore not taxable, or in the alternative it was a revenue receipt, but should have been apportioned over the period during which the work under the contracts would have been performed.

It was held that the sum was chargeable to tax as a receipt in the ordinary cause of the company's trade and must be included in the profits for the accounting period ending on 30th June, 1920 in which it became payable and was in fact paid.[226]

In the case of **CIR v. Fleming & Co**[227] the respondent company carried on business as manufacturers, agents and general merchants. Since before 1903 the company and its predecessors had been sole selling agents in Scotland for certain products of a manufacturer. In 1948 at the instance of the manufacturers the agency was terminated by an agreement under which the company received, *inter alia*, a compensation payment for the loss of the agency. The company contended that the compensation was a capital receipt. The court held that the compensation payment was a trading receipt chargeable to tax.

However, in the case of **Glenboig Union Fireclay Co. v. IRC**[228] the House of Lords held that, a sum received by a company which carried on the business of processing fireclay as compensation for being required to leave unworked the fireclay under a railway was a capital receipt. The

---

[225] 12 TC 955

[226] This decision raises the question of fairness in taxing compensation payments for loss of profits which would have been earned over a number of years in the year of income in which the compensation is paid, especially, where the law does not provide for income averaging.

[227] 33 TC 57

[228] 12 TC 427

payment in this case was made for sterilisation or partial destruction of a capital asset and was not a profit earned in the course of the taxpayer's business or trade. It would not matter if the compensation was determined on the basis of the profits that would have been made by the exploitation of the fireclay. The basis is only the measure of the compensation to be made for the deprivation of the capital asset.

In the earlier discussed case of **CIR v. Flemming** (*supra*) Lord Russel observed that:

> When the rights and advantages surrendered on cancellation of a contract are such as to destroy or materially to cripple the whole structure of the recipient's profit making apparatus, involving the serious dislocation of the normal commercial organisation and resulting perhaps in the cutting down of the staff previously required the recipient of the compensation may properly affirm that the compensation represents the price paid for the loss or sterilisation of a capital asset and is therefore a capital and not a revenue receipt.

But the Fleming decision was upon evidence observed to be elaborately structured so as to absorb such shock. The cancellation contract in that case was only one of eight contracts entered into by the company.

Such was the case in **California Oil Products Ltd v. FCT**.[229] The taxpayer's sole business consisted in acting as the exclusive agent of another company for the sale of its products. The contract under which the taxpayer was appointed contained a restrictive covenant not thereafter to deal in products similar to those of the other company. It agreed to the cancellation of the contract in consideration of the sum of £ 70,000.

The Australian High Court unanimously held that the payments were not profits or income earned in the course of the taxpayer's business. It was observed[230] that the transaction which produced the sum of £70,000 was not an incident in the carrying on of the taxpayer

---

[229] (1934) 52 CLR 28

[230] *Op.Cit.* p.43

company's trade but the relinquishment and abandonment of the only business which the company conducted.[231]

In dealing with cases involving restrictive covenants much depends on the circumstances of the case, but two matters are of special importance in these cases. First is whether the payment is made as an inducement to make substantial alteration in the taxpayer's profit making apparatus. If yes, such payment is likely to be a capital receipt. Second is whether the payment takes the form of (a) recurring payments in which case it is likely to be treated as a trading receipt; or (b) lumpsum payment which may be a capital receipt.

Another area of particular significance in ascertaining profits of a business is the treatment of trading debts. Any monies owing to a taxpayer (carrying on business) at the time of preparing his accounts must be brought to account. Further, section 4 (d) requires that any recovered loss, released liabilities and reserve funds which have become unnecessary must be included in the income of the taxpayer. However, the Commissioner of Income Tax has power to direct, if so requested by the taxpayer in writing, on the modalities of inclusion thereof.[232]

Post Cessation Receipts and Payments

The receipt of income after cessation of business, even in a later year of income, does not mean that it escapes tax whether the recipient has been on a cash basis or an accrual basis.

Sub-section 32 (1) provides that sums received after cessation which, had they been received before, would have been within the scope of income tax are to be included in the income tax computation for the year of income in which the sum is received. If necessary, an additional assessment is raised. Also, if expenditure is incurred after cessation which would have been deductible if incurred before, it may,

---

[231] Read also the East African cases on the point, namely, **Bwavu Mpogoloma Growers' Co-operative Union Ltd. vs. Gaston of Barbons** (1959) EA 307 (CA); **Southern Highlands Tobacco Union Ltd vs. David McQueen** (*supra*); and **Modern Buildings Lts vs. CIT** (1962) EA 275; 3 EATC 337.

[232] Read the cases of **AP Co. Ltd. vs. CIT** 2 EATC 188; and *G.R.* **Mandavia vs. CIT** 2 EATC 426

under sub-section 32 (2) either be deducted in the year of income in which it is paid, or if it cannot be so deducted, it shall be deducted in ascertaining the taxpayer's total income for the year in which such business ceased.[233]

If the cessation of business is, in the case of a company, due to the company being wound up, if the liquidator of such company, in order to effect an economic winding up continues trading on behalf of the company, or where it can be shown that the transactions carried on by him are in the nature of trade, the profits thereof are taxable in the hands of the liquidator as income of the company being wound up. But such receipts should be distinguished from any gains arising from realisation of the company's assets in the normal course of winding up.

Trading Stock and Work-in-Progress

Because the inclusion of trading stock and work-in progress (subsequently referred to as stock) in commercial accounts on a valuation basis can be materially influential upon the results shown by the accounts, the amount at which such stock is brought into the accounts is a very sensitive area from a tax point of view. As a result there are challenges from time to time as to whether a given basis of valuation is valid for tax purposes.

Generally, the treatment for tax purposes follows the accounting treatment but nevertheless there are cases where the method of valuation adopted is not acceptable for tax purposes. For example, the Last In First Out (LIFO) method of valuation was held to be unacceptable in the case of **Minister of National Revenue v. Anaconda American Brass**[234] as was the base stock in **Patrick v. Broadstone Mills**[235] and the replacement value method in **Freeman, Hardy & Willis v. Ridgeway**.[236] The case of **Duple Motor Bodies v. Ostime**[237]

---

[233] The latter could mean that, if necessary, a final assessment is re-opened to admit the deduction.

[234] 34 TC 330

[235] 35 TC 44

[236] 47 TC 519

[237] 39 TC 537

discusses the necessity or otherwise to include overheads in a stock valuation for tax purposes, although this has been largely overtaken by the standard accounting requirements now laid down by the accountancy bodies. In general the Income Tax Department in Tanzania accepts the principles laid down in the guidelines issued by the National Board of Accountants and Auditors (NBAA).

A number of special points arise out of case law in connection with trading stock. For example, the principle in **Sharkey v. Wernher**[238] that where trading stock is appropriated to some other use, perhaps for personal consumption or for use in the business as a fixed asset, it is to be treated as a sale at Fair Market Value (FMV). This situation may also arise in reverse, particularly in connection with real property where a property may have originally been acquired as an investment and is then subsequently appropriated as a current asset with a view to resale.

For example, in the case of **Petrotim Securities v. Ayres**[239] valuable investments held as trading stock were sold to an associate at a nominal price to produce a loss. It was held that this could not constitute a trading transaction and therefore the Fair Market Value must be substituted.

COMPUTATION OF BUSINESS PROFITS

The Income Tax Act, 1973 provides a number of specific circumstances where a given expense is to be deductible and where a given expense cannot be deductible as well as setting out the general rules for deductibility. Therefore, when starting with a profit or loss shown by commercial accounts it is necessary to add back items deducted in arriving at the profit or loss that are not deductible and to deduct those items which are deductible but have not already been deducted in the commercial accounts. Furthermore, in arriving at assessable income it may be necessary to exclude some of the income as not liable to income tax[240] in which case it is necessary to exclude related expenditure

[238] 36 TC 275

[239] 41 TC 389

[240] See sub-section 7 (1) (a) for an example of such exempt income.

and this may involve arbitrary apportionment by the commissioner. In the case of non-residents carrying on business in Tanzania no deduction shall be allowed in respect of any expenditure incurred outside the Partner States other than expenditure which the commissioner determines that adequate consideration has been given.[241] Also in certain special type of business there are specific rules for the ascertainment of total income.[242]

EXEMPT INCOME IN TANZANIA

Section 14 provides that the income specified in the First Schedule to the Act which accrued in or was derived from sources in Tanzania or such other States as may be so specified is exempt from tax to the extent so specified. In addition the following income is also exempt income and has to be excluded in arriving at total income.

1) Profits from the sale of capital assets other than interest in premises or financial assets (section 13);

2) Dividend paid by a resident corporation (sub-section 7 (1) (a));

3) Profits distributed to shareholders by any corporation that is being wound up voluntarily (sub-section 7 (1) (b));

4) Imputed income (sub-section 3 (3));

5) The initial One Hundred and Fifty Thousand Shillings of any income accrued as interest on moneys saved in any bank (sub-section 3 (2) (b); and

6) All such income specified in the First Schedule to the Act.[243]

---

[241] Sub-setion 19 (3) sets out the rules.

[242] For example, insurance business under section 20 of the Act.

[243] Formerly, also exempt was the income of resident persons not arising in or derived from the Partner States (sub-section 3 (1) (a)).

Deductible Expenditure

The general rule for deductibility of expenditure is stated in sub-section 16 (1) as all expenditure incurred "wholly" and "exclusively" for the production of the income sought to be taxed in that year of income.

The terms "wholly" and "exclusively" in that provision refer to two different things. Per Pinson in the case of **Copeman v. Flood**[244] the term "wholly" refers to the quantum of the expenditure, in that, the whole of the expenditure must be for the trade and not only part of it. For example, in the case of **Dollar v. Lyon**[245] a parent operated a farming business. He claimed a deduction for pocket money paid to his children for working on the farm. It was disallowed because the expenditure was not wholly for the purpose of the business because children are expected to work on the family farm for no remuneration.

The term "exclusively" refers to the purpose of the expenditure. For example in the case of **Caillebote v. Quinn**[246] it was held that a self employed person cannot deduct the cost of his food at work because the sole purpose of the food is not trade but also to feed himself.

Principles Used in Determining Whether Expenditure has been Incurred Wholly and Exclusively for the Purpose of Producing Income

The Assessee's Capacity

That is, whether the expenditure is incurred by the assessee in his or her capacity as a trader or whether it is in some other capacity such as a householder, houseowner or some other private capacity not connected with his or her business.

Expenditure incurred on a trading capacity would be presumed to be for the purpose of the trade hence deductible. Mere connection of the expenditure with the trade is not enough. The expenditure must be "incidental" to the business but it need not be "necessary" for the business.

---

[244] (1941) 1 KB 202

[245] 1981 The Times 19th February

[246] (1972) STC 265; (1975) 2 All ER 412. Note also sub-section 17 (2) (a). See also the case of **Union Cold Storage Co. vs. Stones** 8 TC 725 at 741

Commercial Expediency

Whether the expenditure is voluntarily incurred on grounds of commercial expediency. As observed by Viscount Cave, L.J. in the case of **British Insulated and Helsby Cables v. Atherton** (*supra*).

> A sum of money expended, not of necessity and with a view to a direct and immediate benefit to the trade, but voluntarily and on the grounds of commercial expediency and in order indirectly to facilitate the carrying on of the business, may be said to be expended wholly and exclusively for the purpose of trade.

For example, in the case of **Heather v. P.E. Consulting Group Ltd**[247] expenditure to keep employees happy (office parties etc) were held to be deductible as business expenses.[248]

The Subjective Test of Reasonableness

Allowable trading expenses are not subject to the subjective test of reasonableness. Whether an expenditure is incurred for business purpose is a matter of fact to be determined objectively from the circumstances of the expenditure and common business practice.

Business Purpose Test

Whether the direct purpose of the expenditure is to facilitate trade. For example, in the case of **Morgan v. Tate & Lyle Ltd.**[249] the cost of campaign against nationalisation was held to be deductible beause it is an expenditure incurred in preserving the assets of the trader and therefore arises out of trade.[250]

---

247 (1973) Ch. 189

248 Read further discussion of this point in 1979 *British Tax Review* 300

249 (1955) AC 21

250 But in the case of **Bamford vs. A.T.A. Advertisement Ltd.** (1972) 3 All ER 535 deduction of money misappropriated by a director was held not to be a loss arising out of trade because an advertising company does not trade in misappropriation. Read also cases on dual purpose expenditure such as, **Mellalieu vs. Drummond** (1983) 1 WLR 731 which dealt with professional clothing; **Edwards vs. Warmsley** (1968) 1 All ER 1089; and **Bowden vs. Russel** (1965) 2 All ER 258

Production of Assessee's Own Income

Deduction is only allowed for expenditure on the production of the assessee's own income. Thus, for instance, a parent company cannot be allowed a deduction in respect of a loss or business expenditure incurred by or for the purpose of a subsidiary company. Or expenditure by a father to foot electricity bills accumulated by his son's manufacturing company cannot be deducted by him.

Incidental Benefit to a Third Party

Expenditure incurred wholly and exclusively for the purpose of the trader's business will not be disallowed merely because a third party incidentally obtains advantage from the expenditure.[251]

Expenditure for Future Income

It is not necessary that the expenditure allowable in a particular year should result in any profits at all in that year. In the case of **Ward & Co. v. Commissioners of Taxes**[252] it was observed that, in every trade, much of the expenditure in each year such as expenditure in the purchase of raw materials, in repair of plant or the advertisement of goods, is designed to produce results wholly or partially in subsequent years, but, nevertheless, such expenditure is constantly allowed as a deduction for the year in which it is incurred.

Also in the case of **Moore v. Stewarts & Loyd Ltd**[253] it was stated that the expenditure need not result in actual profits to be deductible.[254]

Apart from the general rule as to deductibility contained in sub-section 16 (1), subsetion (2) thereof provides a number of circumstances where certain expenditure is specifically deductible.

---

[251] Read the case of **Wiltshire Brewery Ltd. vs. Bruce** (*supra*)

[252] (1923) AC 145 at 148 (PC)

[253] 6 TC 501 at 507

[254] Read also the East African case of **CIT vs. Overland Co.** 3 EATC 307

NON-DEDUCTIBLE EXPENDITURE

The Income Tax Act, 1973 contains, in section 17 those types of expenses which are not to be deductible for the purpose of ascertaining total income from business for the purposes of income tax and must therefore be added back in arriving at assessable income. These are as follows:

1) Any expenditure or loss which is not wholly and exclusively incurred in the production of income;[255]

2) Any capital expenditure, or any loss, diminution or exhaustion of capital;[256]

3) Any expenditure for personal or domestic purpose;[257]

4) Any expenditure or loss which is recoverable under any insurance contract or indemnity;[258]

5) Any income tax or tax of a similar nature paid on income unless the Act specifically provides otherwise;[259]

6) Contributions to any pension, saving or provident scheme or fund unless the same is specifically allowed under sub-section 16 (2) (n) & (o);[260]

7) Any premium paid under an annuity contract;[261]

8) Any expenditure incurred by a non-resident person not having a permanent establishment in Tanzania in producing income deemed under section 10;[262]

---

[255] Sub-section 17 (1) (a)
[256] Sub-section 17 (1) (b)
[257] Sub-section 17 (2) (a)
[258] Sub-section 17 (2) (b)
[259] Sub-section 17 (2) (c)
[260] Sub-section 17 (2) (d)
[261] Sub-section 17 (2) (e)
[262] Sub-section 17 (2) (f)

(9) Any interest on capital, wages, salary, commission or any other remuneration paid to any partner, or drawings of a partner from the partnership, in the ascertainment of the partnership income.[263]

Apportionments

In other tax jurisdictions there is a general rule that where profits are derived from a business carried on partly in the country of residence or citizenship or domicile, as the case may be, and partly outside such country to apportion the same on a basis as is most reasonable and appropriate in the circumstances.

In Tanzania this rule does not apply. Section 4 (a) provides that where any business is carried on partly within and partly outside Tanzania by a resident person, the whole of the gains or profits from such business shall be deemed to have accrued in or to have been derived from Tanzania.

Trading Losses

Losses are computed in exactly the same way as profits and are deductible under sub-section 16 (4) in ascertaining the total income of that person for the next succeeding year of income.[264]

Accounting Periods

Because commercial and accounting requirements normally dictate that accounts of business profits and losses are made up for periods of account which do not necessarily coincide with the years of income, the Act under section 31 provides for rules for allocating profits and losses of accounting periods to years of income. Also because accounting periods are open to manipulation there is case law aimed to neutralise any changes in accounting period aimed at taking advantage of changes in the rate of tax during a year of income hence reduce tax liability. Currently, however, businesses and individual alike have to structure their financial years to coincide with the calendar year.

---

263 Sub-section 17 (2) (g)

264 Note that under sub-section 16 (4A) this treatment does not apply to a partnership firm.

7

CAPITAL ALLOWANCES

INTRODUCTION

The law governing capital allowances is contained in Sub-section 16 (2) (b) read together with the Second Schedule to the Act. These are allowances which represent the statutory means of allowing for exhaustion of capital expenditure. In effect they replace the depreciation charge in financial accounts, but, the rules governing entitlement to such allowances are highly controlled that some areas of capital expenditure do not qualify for capital allowances. There are broadly five areas of capital expenditure for which separate rules apply in computing capital allowances. These are:

Industrial Buildings;
Machinery;
Mining Operations;
Farm Works; and
Investments.

INDUSTRIAL BUILDINGS

Sub-section 16 (2) (b) read with paragraph 1 in the Second Schedule to the Act allows taxpayers who have incurred capital expenditure on the construction of "industrial buildings" a deduction of such expenditure against income assessable to tax at certain specified rates.

The terms "Industrial Buildings" as defined in paragraph 5 in part 1 of the Second Schedule comprise four main types of Buildings. First, all building connected with some manufacturing or ancillary activity. In particular, buildings which are in use either.

i) For purpose of a business carried on in a mill, factory or similar premises.[265] Although the provision does not contain definitions of the terms a "mill" or "factory", the former generally contain vibrating machinery where something is ground or produced, for example a milling machine. The latter in its Ordinary usage means a place where some goods are produced;[266]

ii) For the purpose of transport undertaking, for example, a railway or bus stations, dock undertaking,[267] a bridge undertaking the use of which is subject to a charge or toll,[268] a tunnel undertaking,[269] inland navigation undertaking such as river navigation, air navigation e.g. an airport hangar, water undertaking as defined under paragraph 5(5) in part 1 of the Second Schedule, an electricity undertaking, that is, an undertaking for the generation, transformation, conversion, transmission or distribution of electrical energy,[270] and an hydraulic power undertaking as defined in paragraph 5(5) thereof; Or

iii) For the purpose of a business which consists of manufacture of goods or material or their subjection to any process;[271] Or

---

[265] Paragraph 5 (1) (a) (i)

[266] Refer the cases of **IRC vs. Leith Harbours and Docks Commissioner** (1942) 24 TC 118; and **Ellerker vs. Union Cold Storage Co. Ltd** (1939) 22 TC 195

[267] The term "dock" is defined in paragraph 5 (5) to include any harbour, wharf, pier or jetty or other works in or at which vessels can ship or unship merchandise or passengers.

[268] See definition of bridge in paragraph 5 (5)

[269] This denotes an underground passage through something tangible like a hill, mountain or even an ocean.

[270] See paragraph 5 (5) thereof

[271] Read the case of **Bourne vs. Norwich Crematorium Ltd.** (1967) 44TC 164

iv) For the business of storage of goods, which are either raw materials, or stored in transit to the market, or to be used in manufacture of certain items, such as shoe laces in shoe manufacturing, or awaiting collection in a warehouse on being imported; and

v) For agriculture, where the business consists of ploughing or cultivating "agricultural land"[272] which is not occupied by the person carrying on the business, or doing any other operation on such land, or threshing the crops of another person.

For example, an owner of agricultural land which is not under cultivation by himself, but, wishing not to sell or lease it engages a contractor who deals in the business of ploughing and cultivating land by modern means for a charge, to so prepare the land for, say, growing maize. If the contractor constructs buildings on the said land for keeping the tractors or storing the threshed crop before delivery to the owner of the land, such buildings are industrial buildings of the contractor.

In addition the Minister can declare any business, for example, an auto repair garage, which does not fit in any of the above categories to be a business to which the provisions of the industrial building deduction can apply.

Second, all buildings concerned with dwelling houses of employees. However, in order for a dwelling house to qualify as an industrial building the following conditions must be satisfied:

a) The taxpayer must carry on a business (any);

b) The taxpayer must have constructed the dwelling houses;

c) Such dwelling houses must be in occupation by the employees of the business of the taxpayer;

d) Such dwelling houses must be prescribed dwelling houses;[273] and

e) Such dwelling houses must conform with such conditions as may be prescribed.

---

[272] As defined in paragraph 22

[273] It appears the Minister of Labour must declare the houses to be prescribed dwelling houses.

The determination of whether a dwelling house is an industrial building for purposes of an industrial building deduction is on an annual basis and on a highly imaginary assumption.

The provision of the proviso to paragraph 5 (3) imposes the test that the dwelling houses in order to be industrial buildings must be such that if the taxpayer owning the dwelling houses ceases to carry on the business whose employees occupy the dwelling houses, such dwelling houses will be either of very little value or no value at all.[274]

The effect of this stringent condition is that, only dwelling houses situated in remote and underdeveloped parts of the country which would be abandoned were the business of the taxpayer to be closed down, such as in a sisal estate, may be eligible to an industrial building deduction.

Third, all buildings connected with the welfare of workers, such as, a canteen, hospital, sports club, gymnasium and the like. Before according them the treatment of industrial building however, it must be shown that:

a) The taxpayer carries on business;

b) The building is in use for the welfare of the workers; and

c) The building will have little or no value at all should the taxpayer cease to carry on business at the end of the year of income.[275]

Fourth, a building which is in use as an hotel or part of an hotel. An hotel is defined under the Hotel Levy Act, 1972[276] to mean any establishment intended for the reception of travellers or visitors who may choose to stay therein, and carried on with a view to profit or gain, but does not include:

i) Any such establishment which has accommodation for less than six guests;

---

[274] Refer the case of **National Coal Board vs. IRC** (1957) 37 TC 264

[275] See proviso to paragraph 5 (3)

[276] Act No. 23 of 1972. See also paragraph 32 (1) in the Second Schedule

ii) Any such establishment which provides sleeping accommodation only; and

iii) Any government rest house.

Paragraph 5 (3) in part 1 in the Second Schedule to the Act is an exclusionary paragraph. It expressly excludes certain buildings from the definition of "industrial building." These are:

1) A retail shop, which is defined under paragraph 5 (5) to include any premises of a similar character where a retail business (including repair work) is carried on.

2) A showroom, which ordinarily means a conspicuous place where goods are kept for display or where customers are attended and briefed on the nature of goods.

3) An office.

Qualifying Expenditure

In order to qualify for relief a person must incur capital expenditure on the construction of a building which is to be an industrial building occupied for the purposes of the business. As regards buildings constructed by the taxpayer himself the capital expenditure, as inferred from paragraph 4 (1) in the Second Schedule, will be the amount actually incurred by him or her on the construction of the building. However, it should be noted that paragraph 1(1) in the Second Schedule implies that mere construction of an industrial building does not by itself entitle a taxpayer to the industrial building deduction in respect of the capital expenditure thereof.

As regards industrial buildings purchased by the taxpayer the capital expenditure on the construction of the building will depend upon the person from whom the building is purchased and upon whether the building is purchased before it is put to first use or after it has been put to first use by the previous owner.

Under paragraph 4 (2) where the building is sold by a person who carries on a business which consists, either in whole or any part thereof, in the construction of buildings with a view to their sale and who sells the building before it is used, in the course of that business, the capital expenditure will be either the amount actually incurred on the construction of the building or the purchase price, whichever is the lesser.[277] The seller of such industrial building cannot claim the deduction because he or she did not put it to first use as required by paragraph 1 (1). If, however, the industrial building is sold after having been put to first use by the seller the taxpayer who subsequently acquires it is not entitled to industrial building deduction.

For example, a person constructs an industrial building to undertake a given project which is frustrated before such building is put to use. Assume the value of the building stood at T.Shs. 1 million after completion. There being no alternative use for the building he disposes of it at T.Shs. 1.20 million to Mr. X a taxpayer who puts the building to use in the business of manufacturing blankets.

According to paragraph 4 (1) (a) the person who constructed the building cannot claim an industrial building deduction because he has never used the building and Mr. X, the taxpayer will under paragraph 4 (1) (b) be allowed an industrial building deduction of only T.Shs. 1 million which is the less amount.

However, if the person who constructed the building was a building contractor, that is, his business was the construction of buildings for sale, the industrial building deduction will under paragraph 4 (2) be the actual price paid by the taxpayer, in this case T.Shs. 1.20 million.

Note that, in case the said building has been sold several times before Mr. X purchased it, then in determining the qualifying capital expenditure only the cost of construction and the last purchase price shall be compared and the lesser of the two amounts shall be allowed as deduction.[278]

Three things should be noted in determining qualifying capital expenditure, namely:

1) Capital expenditure on the construction of a building do not include any capital expenditure on the acquisition of, or of rights in or over, any land.[279]

---

[277] Read paragraph 4 (2) together with paragraph 4 (1) (b)

[278] See the proviso to paragraph 4 (1) (b)

[279] See paragraph 6 (2)

2) Capital expenditure on the construction of a building does not include capital expenditure on the provision of machinery or on any asset which has been treated for any year of income as machinery.[280]

3) Where after the building is constructed capital expenditure is further incurred on repair or extension or renovation of the building the same qualifies for deduction.

Rates of Deduction

The industrial building deduction is given on the cost of the building from year to year. It resembles a straight line method of depreciation deduction and hence remains constant for all the years, except, in the first or the last year if the building is not put to use on the first day of the year of income.

The rates of deduction depend on the nature of the business of the taxpayer and on whether there is an increase in the amount of deduction as provided for in paragraph 1 (1) (a) to (c).[281] However, the rate of deduction shall be reduced if the building is used only for a part of the year.

Residue of Expenditure

This is the balance of the capital expenditure after deductions of all actual industrial building deduction and any notional industrial building deduction (if any). Under paragraph 1 (2) the industrial building deduction can never exceed the residue of expenditure at the end of the year of income before considering the industrial building deduction for that year of income. The mode of determining residue of expenditure is provided in paragraph 3 and it depends on whether the building is used as an industrial building or for non-industrial purposes e.g. office or residence.

---

[280] See paragraph 6 (1)

[281] Under paragraph 31 the Minister has power to increase any deduction in the second schedule where the taxpayer applies to the Commissioner for the increase and satisfies the Commissioner that due to the type of construction of the industrial building or the nature of his business and the use to which the building is put, the life of the industrial building is likely to be substantially less than twenty five years.

For example, a building was constructed at a cost of T.Shs. 1 million on 1/1/92 and put to non-industrial purposes such as an office or residence from 1/7/92. It is subsequently converted into a factory for manufacturing leather goods with effect from 1/4/95. Ascertain the residue of expenditure as at 31/12/96.

		DEDUCTION	SHS
1.	Capital expenditure on construction of the building............................	1,000,000.00	
2.	Vacant from 1/7/92 to 30/6/92	NIL	
3.	Used as office building from 1/7/92 to 31/3/95		
	a) Notional Industrial building deduction at 4% p.a. from 1/7/92 to 31/12/92	20,000.00	20,000.00
	RESIDUE of expenditure as on 31/12/92		980,000.00
	b) Notional Industrial building deduction at 4% p.a. from 1/1/93 to 31/12/93............	40,000.00	40,000.00
	RESIDUE of expenditure as on 31/12/93		940,000.00

c) Notional Industrial Building deduction from 1/7/94 to 31/12/94..........................	40,000.00	40,000.00
RESIDUE of expenditure as on 31/12/94		900,000.00
d) Notional I.B. deduction from 1/1/95 to 31/3/95	10,000.00	
Actual I.B. deduction from 1/4/95 to 31/12/95	30,000.00	40,000.00
RESIDUE of expenditure as on 31/12/95		860,000.00
e) Actual I.B. deduction from 1/1/96 to 31/12/96	40,000.00	40,000.00
RESIDUE of expenditure as on 31/12/96		820,000.00

MACHINERY

As an asset, such as a machine, is used in the production of income it normally either gradually wears out through physical deterioration or gradually becomes obsolete. Since the consequent loss of the investment is gradual, the accounting for the loss occurs over the life of the asset. The principal problems of the depreciation deduction are three. (1) Whether a taxpayer is entitled to a depreciation deduction as respects the particular asset; (2) the determination of the capital investment in the asset that is to be recovered through the deduction; and (3) the determination of the rate of recovery.

Qualifying Persons

The first problem does not cause too much difficult. Paragraph 7 (1) provides that a taxpayer who in a year of income, (i) owns machinery, and (ii) uses such machinery for the purposes of his or her business, shall be entitled to the wear and tear deduction. A lessor of machinery is also, under certain circumstances entitled to wear and tear deduction under paragraph 9.

Machinery

Although the Act uses the term "machinery", it does not, however, define the term "machinery". To make matters worse, there has also been no precise definition of the term by judicial authority. The term "machinery" in a non-technical sense, has a wide meaning and will normally include, for instance, machines with moving parts (whether hand operated or power driven) and mechanical or electrical locomotives.[282]

Qualifying Expenditure

Paragraphs 7 (2) and 8 (1) lay down the rules for determining the capital investment in the asset that is to be recovered through the wear and tear deduction.

The general rule as contained in paragraph 7 (2) is that the wear and tear deduction is upon the written down value of machinery at the end of the relevant year of income.

Meaning of "Written Down Value"

The "written down value" of machinery means the amount still unallowed of the capital expenditure on machinery.[283] However, to determine such an amount one has to look at paragraph 9 of the Management Act[284] which also makes reference to Paragraph 18 in the Second Schedule to the East African Income Tax Act, 1958.[285] The latter provides that:

---

[282] Read the cases of **Yarmouth vs. France** (1887) 19 QBD 647 at 658; **Hinton vs. Maden and Ireland Ltd.** (1959) 3 All ER 356; 38 TC 391; and **A. Co. Ltd. vs. CIT** 1 EATC 1

[283] Paragraph 8 (1)

[284] Cap. 24 of the Community Laws

[285] Act No. 10 of 1958

References in this Part to the amount still unallowed of any capital expenditure as at any time shall be construed as references to the amount of such expenditure less:

a) The initial deduction, if any, made in respect thereof to the person who incurred it; and

b) Any deductions made to such person for any year of income in respect of the machinery on the provision of which he incurred such expenditure under the repealed enactment and the enactments repealed by the repealed enactment together with any such deductions which would have been so made for any other year of income if this Act had always been in force; and

c) Any wear and tear deductions made or deemed to have been made under this schedule in respect of the machinery on the provision of which he incurred such expenditure for any year of income which ended before the time in question; and

d) Any balancing deduction allowed to him in respect of such expenditure;

and this paragraph shall be so construed that any deduction referred to therein shall be made, or deemed to be made, only once in ascertaining the amount still unallowed of any capital expenditure.

Computation of Written Down Value

Paragraph 8 (1) provides for a very intricate legal formula for the computation of written down value on which to allow the wear and tear deduction.

The first step in such computation is to lump together all machinery belonging to the same class. Paragraph 7 (2) classified machinery into three classes, namely:

i) Tractors, combine harvesters, heavy earth-moving equipment and such other heavy self-propelling machines of a similar nature as in his discretion the commissioner, having regard to the likely usage and depreciation in any particular case, may agree;

ii) Other self-propelling vehicles, including aircraft;

iii) All other machinery, including ships.

This is important because the written down value of each class is determined separately. Second, is the determination of costs of any capital expenditure on any machinery of that class. This is normally the purchase price of the machinery plus any deemed purchase price at fair market value (if any).[286]

Third, the following amounts shall be deducted from the said costs of capital expenditure on machinery:

a) Amount realised on the sale of any machinery of that class in the relevant year of income.[287]

b) Any deductions made under Part II of the Second Schedule. These are:

    i) Deduction in respect of capital expenditure on alterations to an existing building in order to install machinery which paragraph 10 deems to be part of the capital expenditure on machinery;

    ii) Deduction in respect of wear and tear deduction in cases where a taxpayer ceases to carry on the business for the purposes of which the machinery was used but who had enjoyed such deduction in the year of income. This deduction

---

286 Note that under paragraph 8 (2) where the taxpayer acquires machinery which he or shie use for the purposes of his or her business without purchasing it, the transaction is, for purposes of wear and tear deduction deemed to be a sale transaction in the open market.

287 Note the 6 years carryback provision in proviso (c) to paragraph 11 (1), that is, where the amount realised for machinery of any class sold in any year of income exceeds that which, but for the deduction of such amoung (see paragraph 11 (1)) would be the written down value of machinery of that calss at the end of such year of income, the excess shall not be deducted but shall be treated as a trading receipt.

is effected in computing the taxpayer's gains or profits for the year of income in which such cessation occurs.[288]

iii) Deduction in respect of a deemed sale under paragraph 8 (2). This occurs where a taxpayer ceases permanently to use machinery which he brought into use for the purposes of his trade, and he does not subsequently sell such machinery.

iv) Deduction in respect of a deemed sale on succession. Paragraph 12 provides that where a person succeeds to any business which until that time was carried on by another person, and machinery which, immediately before the succession was in use for the purposes of the business without being sold is immediately after such succession, in use for the purposes of the business, such machinery shall be deemed to have been sold.

Fourth, the amount still unallowed of any capital expenditure on machinery is determined according to paragraph 18 of the East African Income Tax (Management) Act, 1958 which is quoted above.[289]

The Rates of Deduction

Paragraph 7 (2) sets out different rates for each class of machinery. On machinery of class (i) the wear and tear deduction equals 37.5 per cent of the written down value of machinery for that class. Machinery of class (ii) qualifies for a 25 per cent deduction and those of class (iii) a 12.5 percent deduction.

---

[288] See paragraph 11 (1). Note that the same sub-paragraph provides that in ceases the taxpayer cases to carry on business and the wear and tear deduction is exhausted, if, in the year of income in which he ceases to carry on business the fully depreciated machinery still have some useful life, its fair market value thereof shall constitute a balancing charge which shall be deemed to be income subject to tax under section 4 (e)

[289] Note however, where there is a non-arm's length transaction or some collusive agreement aimed at influencing the above computation, paragraph 13 empowers the Commissioner to neutralise any such arrangement. In additon, paragraph 14 gives him apportionment power where machinery is also put ot private use.

MINING OPERATIONS

Paragraph 17 provides for deduction in respect of expenditure incurred in any year of income on mining operations.[290]

Definition of Expenditure

The term "expenditure" as used in this paragraph is defined under paragraph 16 (1) to mean the sum of prospecting capital and development capital expenditure, incurred in the United Republic of Tanzania by any person carrying on mining operations and any amount of additional capital allowance computed for the year of income in accordance with the provisions of paragraph 18.

Qualifying Persons

The mining operation deduction is allowed to three categories of taxpayers, namely:

1) Persons who carry on mining operations;[291]

2) Transferees of assets representing expenditure in respect of which the transferor is entitled to a deduction under paragraph 17. However, such transferee will only be entitled to a reasonable portion of the deduction, as shall be determined by the Commissioner.[292]

---

290 Note that, before the amendment to Part III in the second schedule effected by the Finance Act, 1997 (Act No. 27 of 1997)the qualifying expenditure was in respect of capital expenditure.

291 See paragraph 17. Also note that the term "mining" is defined in sub-section 2 (1) to mean, intentionally winning minerals and includes every method or process by which any mineral is won. The terms "mining operations" is also defined under the said sub-section as meaning, prospecting, mining or operations connected with prospecting or mining carried out pursuant to rights granted under the Mining Act, 1979. The term "Mineral" is defined under sub-section 2 (1) as any substance, whether in solid, liquid, or gaseous form, occurring naturally in or on the earth, or in or under the seabed, formed by or subject to a geological process, but does not include petroleum as defined in the Petroleum (Exploration and Production) Act, 1980, or water.

292 See paragraph 19 (a) & (b)

3) A purchaser of assets representing expenditure in respect of which a deduction is allowed under paragraph 17, and who carries on mining operations. The purchaser shall for the purposes of the deductions on mining operations be deemed to have incurred prospecting capital expenditure or, as the case may be, development capital expenditure.[293]

Qualifying Expenditure

Paragraph 17 provides for the expenditure which qualifies for deduction in ascertaining the gains or profits of a person who in any year of income carries on mining operations. As a general rule, the whole amount representing such expenditure is deductible. According to the definition of the term "expenditure" for mining operations deduction purposes,[294] the qualifying expenditure relates to three things:

1) ***Prospecting Capital Expenditure: (PCE)***

   This is capital expenditure incurred wholly and exclusively for the purpose of prospecting and includes expenditure incurred in the acquisition of rights in or over deposits of minerals. The process of ascertainment of the quantum of the PCE is rather evidentiary. In other words, proof of expenditure is required before it is admitted and included as part of expenditure envisaged under paragraph 17.

2) ***Development Capital Expenditure***

   This is capital expenditure incurred wholly and exclusively for the purpose of development operations. Development operations in this regard means operations carried out for or in connection with the development of a mine and includes operations to add, to alter or improve an existing mine.[295]

3) ***Additional Capital Allowance***

   This is a capital allowance which is allowed to be added upon the sum of (1) plus (2) above in order to make up the qualifying expenditure.

---

[293] Paragraph 20

[294] Paragraph 16 (1)

[295] Paragraph 16 (1)

The definition of the term "expenditure" under paragraph 16 (1) specifically excludes the following expenditure:

a) Any expenditure on the acquisition of the site of deposits of minerals or the site of buildings or works, or of right in or over such site; and

b) Any expenditure on works constructed wholly or mainly for subjecting raw products of such deposits to any process except a process designed for preparing the raw product for use as such.

Ascertainment of items (1) and (2) which constitute a part of the deductible expenditure does not pose any problems. These are usually vouchered expenditure items. The Commissioner, however, has to ascertain compliance with the "wholly and exclusively" rule before admitting the same in computing the expenditure.

The ascertainment of item (3), that is, the additional capital allowance to be included in computing the expenditure is subject to intricate rules provided for under paragraph 18.

Computation of the Additional Capital Allowance

The additional capital allowance is computed on qualifying capital expenditure. That is, the development capital expenditure net of prospecting capital expenditure or any interest or financial charges.[296]

The allowance is computed as a percentage of the unredeemed qualifying capital expenditure. Paragraph 18 (1) provides for fifteen percentum. The terms "unredeemed capital expenditure" refers to the amount of the qualifying capital expenditure which could not be deducted against the available income in any particular year of income and is reflected as part of any deficit brought forward.

According to paragraph 18 (1) the deficit brought forward is allowed as a deduction for the qualifying person at the commencement of each year of income.

The computation of the additional capital allowance for the succeeding years of income is upon accumulated qualifying capital expenditure. Under paragraph 18 (3) the accumulated qualifying capital

---

[296] Paragraph 18 (2)

expenditure in relation to a mine is ascertained at the end of the year of income and provides the allowance base for the application of the additional capital allowance. The allowance base is the sum of:

a) Unredeemed qualifying capital expenditure brought forward from the year preceding the year of income;

b) Plus the additional capital allowance calculated thereon;

c) Plus qualifying capital expenditure incurred during the year of income;

d) Minus any such qualifying capital expenditure set off against the income of another mine;

e) Minus gains or profits chargeable to tax in relation to such mine for the year of income calculated before any deduction in respect of qualifying capital expenditure and including any proceeds of disposal of assets previously included as qualifying capital expenditure.

Sub-paragraphs (4) to (7) and paragraph 21 inclusive provide for restrictions in the application of the additional capital allowance.[297]

EXPENDITURE ON AGRICULTURAL LAND

Paragraph 22(1) of Part IV of the Second Schedule allows a deduction in respect of capital expenditure on the construction of farm works.

Qualifying Persons

Only two categories of taxpayers can claim farming deduction. Such taxpayer must be, either an owner or tenant of any agricultural land,[298] or a transferee of interest in agricultural land where the transferor is an owner or tenant of the transferred agricultural land who would have been entitled to farming deduction but for such transfer.

---

[298] Paragraph 22 (1)

"Agricultural land" is defined in paragraph 23 to mean land occupied wholly or mainly for the purposes of a trade of husbandry. Note that the term "husbandry" also includes other allied activities incidental to the business of farming.

Qualifying Expenditure

The farming deduction in paragraph 22 is in respect of capital expenditure incurred in any year of income on the construction of "farm-works." Paragraph 23 defines "farm works" to mean farmhouses, labour quarters, any other immovable buildings necessary for the proper operation of the farm, fences, dips, drains, water and electricity supply works other than machinery, windbreaks and other works necessary for the proper operation of the farm. The definition as almost all-embracing.

In addition to expenditure on the construction of farm works, paragraph 22(3)(b) also extends the farming deduction where capital expenditure is incurred on any assets other than a farmhouse, which asset is to serve partly the purposes of husbandry and partly other purposes. However, the farming deduction to be allowed in such a case is to be determined by the Commissioner in a manner he considers to be just and reasonable.

Rates of Deduction

The farming deduction is allowed in the year of income in which the qualifying expenditure is incurred and in the four following years of income at the rate of one-fifth of such expenditure.[299] In addition, paragraph 22(3) provides that where the expenditure is on a farmhouse, one-third only of such expenditure shall be taken into account unless the Commissioner, considering the accommodation and amenities of the farm house in relation to the natrure and extent of the farm decides on a lesser proportion thereof.[300] Further, where the expenditure is incurred on any assets other than a farmhouse, which asset is to serve partly the purposes of husbandry and partly other purposes, then the

---

[299] *Ibid.*

[300] Paragraph 22 (3) (a)

deduction shall be restricted to only such proportion thereof as the Commissioner may determine to be just and reasonable.

Note the prohibition in paragraph 22(2) that no capital expenditure shall be taken into account unless it is incurred for the purposes of husbandry on the agricultural land in question.

An Illustration

Consider a taxpayer engaged in the business of animal and crop husbandry on agricultural land and who incurs the following capital expenditure on the construction of farm works:

1) Construction of an ordinary farmhouse on 1/10/89 .... 30,000.00

2) Construction of water supply works on 1/10/89 .... 30,000.00

3) Installation of an electric water pump on 1/10/89 .... 20,000.00

4) Construction of electricity supply works on 18/11/89 .... 80,000.00

5) Installation of an electricity generator on 18/11/89 ....100,000.00

6) Construction of a garage to house a tractor on 28/11/89 .... 40,000.00

7) Purchase of a tractor on 28/11/89 .... 160,000.00

8) Purchase of a second hand car on 28/11/89 .... 36,000.00

   (N.B.: The land space occupied by the car is only 1/3 of total space of the garage).

9) Construction of a stable to keep 100 herds of cattle on 7/12/89.... 30,000.00

10) Purchase of cattle @ Shs. 500/= each on 7/12/89 .... 50,000.00

Assume the following information concerning the taxpayer is discovered by the tax authorities:

a) That 2% of total water consumption on the farm is private use;

b) That 5% of total electricity consumption on the farm is private us;

c) That 1/3 of the motorcar use is personal use;

d) That 1% of milk products of the cattle is consumed privately;

e) That all the remaining uses of the above items is proved by the taxpayer to be solely in respect of his business of animal and crop husbandry.

Assuming further that the taxpayer started his farming business on 1/10/89. Calculate all the capital deductions admissible to the farmer for the year of income 1989.

Answer:

Part II - Wear and Tear Eduction For 1989

A. **Machinery:**

	Class I (37.5%)	Class II (25%)	Class III (12.5%)
	(Shs.)	(Shs.)	(Shs.)
Opening written down value	NIL	NIL	NIL

Add:			
Purchases (28/11/89)	160,000.00	(28/11/89) 36,000.00	(1/10/89) 20,000.00 (18/11/89) 100,000.00
	160,000.00	36,000.00	120,000.00
Less: Sales	NIL	NIL	NIL
Written down value before considering wear and tear for 1989	160,000.00	36,000.00	120,000.00
Wear and tear for year of income 1989	60,000.00	9,000.00*	15000.00**
Written down value as at 31/12/89	100,000.00	27,000.00	105,000.00

Notes:

* Since the motor-car is used to the extent of 1/3 for private use the same proportion of the deduction as worked out above will be disallowed under paragraph 14 and only 2/3 of the deduction i.e. 6,000.00 will be allowed in computing the taxpayers total income in respect of class II.

** Similarly wear and tear deduction on the water pump will be reduced by 2% under paragraph 14; And 5% of the generator wear and tear will also be reduced under paragraph 14.

i.e. (2% of 20,000 x 12.5%) = 50.00 +
(5% of 100,000 x 12.5%) = 625.00
: 15,000.00 - 675.00 = 14,735.00

(Wear and tear to be allowed on class III).

Part IV Deductions

B. Farm Works

Determination of Qualifying Expenditure	Year of Income 1989 (Shs.)
1. **Farmhouse** - Normal farmhouse at 30,000.00 Qualifying expenditure under paragraph 22(3)(a) = 1/3	10,000.00
2. **Water Supply Works** Cost = 30,000.00 less 2% private consumption under paragraph 22(3((a) = 600.00	29,400.00
3. **Electricity Supply Works** Cost = 80,000.00 less 5% personal consumption disallowed under paragraph 22(3)(b) = 4,000.00	76,000.00
4. **Garage** Cost = 40,000.00. Since 1/3 of total land space is occupied by the motor car, 1/3 of the total cost is atrributable to the motor car i.e. 13,333.00 and balance of the cost attributable to tractor. Further, since 1/3 of use of motor car is private, 1/3 of the cost is attributable to motor car (13,333.00) i.e. 4,444.00 must be reduced. Therefore only the balance of Shs. 8,889.00 is eligible deduction. Qualifying expenditure is therefore (26,667 + 8,889)	35,556.00
[i.e. (40,000 - 4,444) or (40,000 - 13,333) + 8,889)]	

5. **Stable**

Cost = 30,000.00. Since 1% of milk products used privately, 1% of total cost must be reduced under paragraph 22(3)(b) i.e. 30,000 - (30.000 x 1%) = 300	29,700.00
Total qualifying expenditure	180,656.00
Farming deduction = 1/5 of the qualifying expenditure =	36,131.00

C. **Summary of Capital Deductions Allowable Under the Second Schedule for the Year of Income 1989.**

	Part II Deductions (Shs.)	Part IV Deductions (Shs.)
Machineries		
Class I	60,000.00	
Class II	6,000.00	
Class III	14,325.00	
Frame Works		
		36,131.00
	80,325.00	36,131.00

: Total = Shs. 116,456.00

INVESTMENT DEDUCTIONS

The main object of investment deductions is to give direct tax investment to entrepreneurs who are ready to risk their capital in specified investments. The deductions is given as an additional capital deduction.

Qualifying Persons

There is under paragraphs 24, 24A, 25 and 26 in Part V of the second schedule a wide range of persons who qualify for investment deduction.

Paragraph 24 alone has about seven categories of taxpayers who can claim investment deduction. These are:

1) Taxpayers who incur qualifying expenditure as defined in Part I of the Second Schedule on the construction of an industrial building which is to be used by him or by a lessee for the purposes of an approved business.

   Note that an "Approved Business" is defined under paragraph 32(1) to mean a business declared by the Minister by notice in the Gazette to be an approved business for the purposes of the grant of investment deduction.[301]

   The Minister has issued such Notice[302] in which approved business comprise every trade or business which consists in the manufacture of goods or materials to any process.[303]

2) Taxpayers who incur capital expenditure on the purchase of machinery which has been installed and is used solely in an industrial building for the purposes of an approved business.

3) A taxpayer who is a lessee of an industrial building, if he incurs qualifying expenditure, as defined in Part II of the Second Schedule, on the purchase of machinery which has been installed and is solely used in that building, or which is to be installed or solely used in the industrial building for the purposes of an approved business.[304]

4) A taxpayer who incurs qualifying capital expenditure as defined in Part I of the Second Schedule on the construction or extension of a building which is subsequently used as an hotel.

---

[301] See *Income Tax (Approved Business) Declaration Notice, 1978* in Government Notice No. 86 of 1978 which has a retrospective effect to January 1, 1974

[302] *Ibid.*

[303] The term "manufacture" is defined in sub-section 2 (1) of the *National Industries (Licensing and Registration) Act, 1967* Act No.10 of 1967

[304] Cost of machinery is defied under paragraph 32 (4)

Note, however, such taxpayer will only qualify for the investment deduction such construction or extension of such building, is certified by the Minister.

5) A taxpayer who incurs capital expenditure on the purchase of machinery which has been installed and is used solely in an hotel.

6) A taxpayer who is an owner or lessee of a non-industrial building and who has incurred, after January 1, 1974, qualifying capital expenditure on the purchase of machinery which has been installed and is used solely in such building for the purposes of an approved business. Note that, such expenditure should not be on substantially replacing old machinery previously in use in an existing business of such owner or lessee.

7) A taxpayer who incurs qualifying capital expenditure, as defined in Part IV of the Second Schedule, on the establishment of or investment in an agricultural or livestock development farm.

8) Paragraph 24A provides that a taxpayer who is an owner or a tenant of any agricultural land used for the purposes of husbandry will be entitled to investment deduction if he or she incurs qualifying capital expenditure on:

   a) The construction of or extension to any immovable building on such land which was erected for the purpose of:

      i) Processing in any way the produce of such land or of any livestock,

      ii) Storing feeds, fertilizers, insecticides, inputs, agricultural produce before or after processing,

      iii) Providing accommodation for livestock held on such land

   b) The installation of any power or water supply for irrigation including boreholes and water conservation;

c) The clearing of land not previously cultivated or previously neglected or abandoned and the planting thereon of permanent or semi-permanent crops.

Section 2(1) defines "permanent or semi-permanent crops" to mean crops declared by the Minister by a notice in the Gazette to be permanent or semi-permanent crops.

9) Paragraph 25 provides for an investment deduction in respect of ship to any taxpayer who is a resident person carrying on the business of a ship owner, who purchases a power-driven ship of more than 495 tons, which is new, or if used, it has been refitted by the taxpayer at a cost which at least equals 25 percent of the total cost of the ship.

Note, however, the ship investment deduction shall not be available to such taxpayer if investment deduction has been given in respect of the same ship to any other taxpayer in Tanzania, or if the ship has been sold by the taxpayer to anyone within five years of the end of the year of income in which it was first used by him or her.

10) The purchaser of an industrial building[305]

Quantum of Investment Deduction

In respect of buildings and machinery, paragraph 24 provides for an investment deduction of 20 per cent of the capital expenditure incurred by the taxpayer in respect of either the qualifying industrial building or machinery or both, as the case may be. However, the Minister, may under paragraph 31 increase the quantum of the deduction, but, he has no power to decrease such quantum. The same quantum applies to hotels. In respect of a ship, the investment deduction is equal to 40 percent of the capital expenditure on the total purchase price of the ship and the cost of refitting if any.

---

[305] See paragraphs 26 and 4

Modus of Claiming Investment Deduction

The deduction can only be claimed in the year of income in which the qualifying asset is put to first use. However, under paragraph 24(1) a taxpayer may elect the year or years in which the investment deduction can be claimed by him. This means the taxpayer can either:

a) Claim the whole of the investment deduction in the year of income in which the qualifying asset is first put to use; or
b) Claim the whole of the investment deduction in any subsequent year of income; or
c) Claim the investment deduction partly in the year of income in which the asset is first put to use and partly in any one or any number of subsequent years of income; or
d) Claim the investment deduction partly in the year of income subsequent to the year of income in which the qualifying asset is put to first use and partly in subsequent years of income in such quantities as he may like.

Reference Cases

On Industrial Building Deduction

1. **IRC v. Leith Harbours and Docks Commissioners** (1942) 24 TC 118.
2. **Ellerker v. Union Cold Storage Co. Ltd.** (1939) 22 TC 195.
3. **Bourne v. Norwich Crematorium Ltd.** (1967) 44 TC 164.
4. **National Coal Board v. IRC** (1957) 37 TC 264.
5. **Kimarnock Equitable Cooperative Society Ltd v. IRC** (1966) 42 TC 675.
6. **IRC v. Lambhill Iron Works Ltd.** (1950) 31 TC 393.
7. **Abbot Laboratories Ltd v. Carmody** (1968) 2 All ER 879.

On Farming Deduction

8. **CIT v. Kagera Saw Mills Ltd.** (1972) EA 387 (CA).
9. **CIT V. Kiganga Estates Ltd.** (1968) EA 464.

On Investment Deduction

10. **CIT v. Ajay Printers Ltd.** 58 ITR 811.
11. **CIT v. Gopal** 58 ITR 598.
12. **Commissioner General of Income Tax v. P. Ltd.** (1970) EA 328 (CA).
13. **Burmah Shell Refineries Ltd. v. Chaud** 61 ITR 493.
14. **CIT v. B. Ltd.** (1973) EA 322 (K).
15. **U. Ltd v. CIT** (1973) EA 315 (K).
16. **CIT v. I.A. Ltd.** (1973).
17. **Winnipeg v. Brian Investment** (1953) 1 D.L.R. 270.
18. **S. Ltd v. CIT** (1973) EA 448.

8

TAXATION OF CAPITAL GAINS

INTRODUCTION

Capital gains and losses are nothing more than of form of profit or loss from a particular sources, namely, the disposition of property in a capital transaction i.e. a transaction the profit or loss from which is not included in or deducted from a taxpayer's income as "ordinary" income or loss from office or employment, business or property or another source.

Before 1973 capital gains or profits from the sale or other disposal of property otherwise than in the course of business were not income for tax purposes. The East African Income Tax (Management) Act 1958[306] as well as the East African Income Tax Management Act, 1971[307] levied no tax on capital gains.

The basis of exclusion of such gains from the ambit of income taxation was the accepted principle that income tax is a tax on income and not capital and, therefore, as authoritatively stated in the case of **California Copper Syndicate v. Harris**,[308] proceeds from disposition of capital

[306] Act No. 10 of 1958

[307] Cap. 24 of Community Laws

[308] (*supra*)

asset do not constitute income for purposes of taxation. Several other English cases maintained the same position.[309] In East Africa the courts also maintained that capital gains were outside the purview of income tax law.[310]

Capital gains were first brought within ambits of Tanzania income taxation by sections 3(2)(e) read with sections 13 and 33(3) of the Income Tax Act, 1973. Several factors account for this changed attitude. First and foremost the recognition in many tax jurisdictions of the principle of "a buck is a buck is a buck ...", that is, a taxpayer who realises a capital gain of say T.Shs. 1,000/= is in the same position as a taxpayer who earns T.Shs. 1,000/= from employment. Thus it is only fair and equitable to tax capital gains.

Second, is the need to curb tax avoidance. By taxing capital gains the incentive for taxpayers to structure their transactions to look like capital transactions rather than income producing transactions is reduced. For example, the fact that capital gains were tax free encouraged shareholders in companies with substantial accumulated surpluses to sell their shares rather than take out the surplus in the form of dividends because the gain on the sell of shares was a tax free gain whereas the dividends were tax able income.

Third it was argued that capital gains tax would assist to combat speculation in property and encourage serious capital investment.

SCOPE OF THE CAPITAL GAINS TAX

Section 13 (1) defines capital gains to mean the difference between the value of consideration for which an asset or a financial asset is sold and so much of the adjusted cost to the taxpayer of such interest or financial asset as has not been claimed as deduction in respect of the capital expenditure to such interest or such financial asset under the second schedule.

---

[309] See the cases of **CIR vs. Livingstone** 11 TC 542; and **Leeming vs. Jones** 15 TC 33; and **Edwards vs. Barristow & Harrison** 36 TC 207

[310] See the cases of **Y. Co.Ltd vs. CIT** 2 EATC 50; **CIT vs. Sydney Tate** (*supra*); **H. Co. Ltd. vs. CIT** 1 EATC 65 and **AL vs. CIT** 2 EATC 148. Read also the cases of **London County Council vs. AG** (1901) AC 26; **Green vs. British Salmon** 22 TC 29; **Secretary of State for India vs. Scobble** (1903) AC 299; **Eisner vs. Macomber** (1919) 252 US 189; and **CIT vs. Shaw Wallace** (1932) Camp. Cas. 276

Persons Chargeable

All persons, natural or artificial are chargeable to a capital gains tax on chargeable dispositions unless specifically exempted under section 14 and the First Schedule to the Act.

Chargeable Assets

Section 13(1) restricts the charge to capital gains tax to interest in premises and financial assets. The term "premises" is defined under section 2(1) to mean land and any improvements thereon, and includes any building or, where part of a building is occupied as a separate dwelling house, that part. The Act is silent as to what "financial asset" means. Initially, the tax extended to motor vehicles, but these were removed from its scope by the Finance Act, 1976. Thus, all other capital assets are not chargeable assets for the purposes of capital gains tax.

This discrimination apparently creates problems of equity, in particular, horizontal equity. For example, a person who sells his or her jewellery at T.Shs. 10,000/= has the same capability as another who sells a plot of land at the same T.Shs. 10,000/=. Under the Act the latter will suffer a tax whereas the former will enjoy his or her scoop tax-free.

Chargeable Dispositions

In this respect, as well, the Act is very restrictive. The capital gains tax is levied only where the chargeable asset is disposed of by way of sale. Note that, disposition can take several forms. For example, exchange, conveyance, gift, compulsory acquisition with compensation, relinquishment, bequeath and many other forms.

In other tax jurisdictions the term used is wide enough to cover any form of disposition, and imputation rules are used to bring any person to the charge of tax. For example, the Kenyan legislation uses the term "transfer" instead of "sell." The Indian Act also uses the same term. Under English law the term used in "disposal" which also carries a very wide meaning.

The use of the term "sell" in the Act restricts the tax to sale transactions. This opens a vent for taxpayers to disguise their transactions in order to avoid the tax. For example, where a person bequeaths his land to his son or dependant, or transfers the land to his friend as a wedding gift, the gain therefrom will attract no capital gains tax, unless the Commissioner invokes section 27 to declare the transaction as one designed to avoid or evade tax. In Canada, by comparison, such a gain would be imputed to the transferor of the asset and taxed on him/her.

The Charging Procedure

Sub-section 13 (1) (a) and (b) provides that to determine a capital gain which should be subject to tax, one has to compute and ascertain:

i) Selling price;

ii) The adjusted cost of the asset to be deducted from the selling price;

iii) Ascertain the excess and levy a capital gains tax at the rate prescribed.[311]

Determination of the Selling Price

Formerly no guidance was offered by the Act on how to determine the selling price i.e. whether the selling price should be the fair market value (FMV) of the asset or the actual consideration paid under the agreement for sale. If the latter should be the selling price, it creates room for collusion by the parties to cheat the tax authorities.

However, this anomaly was previously to an extent cured by the amendment to section 13(4) effected by the Finance Act 1983. That is, for the purposes of assessing capital gains tax, the valuation of premises was to be determined in accordance with the directions by the Minister specified in the Gazette. In practice, the Commissioner required the vendor of interest in premises to produce a valuation report prepared by a Government Valuer and will normally rely on the value disclosed therein.

Further, section 13(5) gave the commissioner a first option to purchase the asset if in his opinion the asset had been under valued or the price understated. The option, however, had to be exercised within not more than ninety days from the date the seller submitted his return

---

[311] See sub-section 33 (3) read with the 3rd schedule to the Act.

for the purposes of capital gains tax assessment. The re-enactment of the capital gains tax by the Finance Act 1999 fell short of re-enacting sub-sections 13 (4) and (5). Whereas under the previous sub-sections one could safely assume that the selling price should be the asset's fair market value, it is difficult to make such an assumption under the new section 13.

Determination of Cost

The Act lack clarity in this respect. It is not clear whether the adjusted cost in section 13(1)(b) is to be worked out from the price of acquisition or the asset's total cost before sale. Under the Kenyan legislation, cost of an asset comprise the price of acquisition plus any amount expended wholly and exclusively for enhancing or preserving value of the asset, or defending title or right over it, incidental cost for effecting acquisition, such as, fees or commission to professional valuer, agent or other professional advisor, stamp duty, registration fee, advertising expenses and any other expense which the department may allow.

Method of Taxing Capital Gains

Capital gains are chargeable to tax in the year of realisation although the gains will have accrued gradually over the holding period. This in a way creates a problem of hidden tax because the cost is computed in historical shillings while the selling price is in current shillings. With the prevalent currency fluctuation and inflation the nominal gain so computed exceeds the real gain to the taxpayer.

The Rates of Capital Gains Tax

The rate of the capital gains tax is provided for under item 7 in the 3rd schedule to the Act. This is a single flat rate of ten percent.

Treatment of Capital Losses

Unlike trading losses which are allowable deductions under sub-section 16 (4), capital losses are not so allowed. It would be fair and just if the Act were to be amended to provide for the deduction of capital losses against other capital gains realised by the taxpayer in other disposals in that year or subsequent years of income or even set-off from other ordinary income.

9

THE TAXATION OF INTERMEDIARIES

INTRODUCTION

Most business is conducted through legal entities such as partnership firms, corporations, trusts and other associations. These entities are also used to hold property. The existence of such entities have varying tax implications. Some of the entities constitute independent taxpayers, some are mere *conduct pipes* but to certain extent recognised as independent persons for certain purposes of income taxation.

PARTNERSHIP

The Act does not define what the term "partnership" means. However, it does define a "partnership firm" to mean a firm of two or more persons carrying on business in partnership.

In the case of **E v. CIT**[312] it was observed that whether or not a partnership exists is a question of fact. The existence of a deed of partnership and of the requisite registration is not conclusive, but contrarywise, the absence of such documents might imperil a claim that a partnership does exist. The court in this case made reference to the definition of a partnership in section 239 of the Indian contract

[312] 1 EATC 30

Act, that:

> Partnership is the relation which subsists between persons who have agreed to combine their property, labour or skill in some business and to share the profits thereof between them.

A partnership is, therefore, a mere relation and can never be a person. But for purposes of income taxation to a certain extent a partnership is accorded the status of a legal person independent from the partners. Under section 4 (b) income of the partnership is determined at the level of the firm, in order to later on determine the gains or profits of a partner from the firm. To that extent the firm is treated separately from the partners. Until 1985, the firm was also taxed on its income before its profits are distributed to the partners. The same income suffered tax again in the hands of the partners at the individual level. However, the Finance Act 1985 (July) deleted the partnership rate of tax provided for under sub-section 33 (1) (b) and the Third Schedule to the Act. Therefore, a partnership firm is a mere conduit for income tax purposes.

PARTNERS' GAINS OR PROFITS

A partnership firm is a business entity. The business of the firm is essentially that of its partners. It follows that gains or profits of a partner from the firm constitute business income subject to tax under sub-section 3 (2) (a) (i). Section 4 (b) sets forth the rules of determining gains or profits of a partner from a partnership. These are:

a) Any remuneration payable to him by the partnership;

b) Any interest on capital payable to him by the partnership net of any interest on capital which the partner way have paid to the partnership;

c) His/her share of the total income or loss of the partnership.

It should be noted that, because income of a partnership derive from business, all the rules discussed in chapter four herein, as regards the taxation of income from business as well apply in ascertaining the total income of the partnership firm.

DETERMINATION OF PARTNERSHIP

Being a relationship, a partnership may be determined by either demise of a partner, retirement of a partner or even addition of a new partner. Anything which causes the constitution of a partnership firm to be altered may put an end to the firms existence. In other tax jurisdictions, in order to prevent abuse of this entity by tax avoiders complex rollover and attribution rules have evolved. For example, where a new partner joins a partnership firm, the property of the old firm automatically rolls over to the new firm created by the addition of the new member, and the cost base of the partnership interests of each member is adjusted to take count of the new relationship. There are no such provisions in the Income Tax Act, 1973. Apparently the only relevant provision in the event of the determination of partnership is section 32 which caters for income and expenditure after cessation of business.

Trusts

The Act does not define the term "trust", but it does define the term "trustee" to include an executor of a will of a deceased and an administrator of an estate of the deceased.[313] It further provides that "trustees" for the purposes of the Act shall be deemed to be a body of persons.[314] A reference to a trust is in fact not a reference to the trust at all, but. instead a reference to the trustees and others, such as, heir and other legal representative having ownership or control of the trust property, on whom the Act imposes tax with respect to the income of the trust.

Settlement of Trust

There are two major kinds of trusts, namely, "testamentary" trusts and "inter vivos" trusts. The former is one which arises on the death of an individual and was created by him. All the other trusts are "inter vivos" trusts. For example, settlements whereby income is paid by the settler[5] to or for the benefit of a child.[315]

---

[313] Sub-section 2 (1)

[314] *Ibid.*

[315] See sub-section 29 (7) (a) & (c)

Residence of a Trust

Since trustees are treated as a body of persons, their residence shall be determined according to the rules laid down under sub-section 2 (2) (c), that is, the trust shall be resident where the management and control of such trust is exercised during any period in a year of income. If there is only one trustee then his or her residence shall be that of an individual as provided for under section 2 (2) (a).

Income of Trust

The income of a trust is chargeable to tax in the hands of the trustee or trustees. This is because section 11(1) provides that any income chargeable to tax under the Act and received by any person in his capacity as a trustee shall be deemed to be income of such trustee.

This provision appears to modify the old principle that income of a trust should only be assessed on a trust and no other person. There are several East African cases upholding this principle which were decided prior to the enactment of the Act. For example, the case of **AD v. CIT**[316] and **AG v. CIT.**[317] In both cases the taxpayers had created trusts which were used to accumulate income and avoid tax. The Commissioner sought to assess the trustees instead of the trusts. The court in both cases maintained that only the trusts are assessable to tax. However, were these cases to be decided today, the courts would have upheld the Commissioner's decision on the basis of section 11(1).

Income of Beneficiary

A "beneficiary" is a person beneficially interested in a trust. Sub-section 11 (2) provides that any amount received in any year of income by a person beneficially entitled thereto from any trustees or which is paid out of trust income by the trustee on behalf of such person is deemed to be income of the beneficiary.[318]

---

[316] 2 EATC 89

[317] 2 EATC 113

[318] In such a case the tax (if any) paid by the trustee on such income becomes deductible under section 41 (b)

In ascertaining the income of a beneficiary from the trust a deduction must be made, in the case other than that of an annuity directed to be paid free of tax,[319] of the tax already paid by the trustee on such income. However, if the amount paid to the beneficiary is an annuity directed to be paid free of tax, the income of the beneficiary shall be the gross amount of such annuity plus the amount of sums paid by such trustee to the beneficiary for the purposes of meeting his liability to tax on such annuity.

Note, however, a beneficiary who is beneficially entitled to a trust under a will or on intestacy and who receives any amount from an executor or an administrator is under certain circumstances exempt from tax on any such amount. The proviso to sub-section 11 (2) deems such amount not to be chargeable income in the hands of such beneficiary if the same is paid to him after a tax at the administration rate has been paid on such amount.

TAX TREATMENT OF SETTLEMENTS

A "settlement" is defined under sub-section 29 (7) to include any disposition, trust, covenant, agreement, arrangement, or transfer of assets, but does not include any of the foregoing if they result from an order of a court unless such order is made in contemplation of this provision. Sub-section 30 (5) further excludes from the definition of the term "settlement:"

i) A settlement made for valuable and sufficient consideration; and

ii) Any agreement made by an employer to confer a pension upon an employee in respect of any period after the cessation of employment or to provide an annual payment for the benefit of the widow or any relative or dependant of such employee after his death, or to provide a lump sum to an employee on the cessation of such employment.

However, this further exclusion in sub-section 30 (5) should be read in the context of the provisions of section 30.

[319] See sub-section 35 (1) (c). Read also section 54

Settlements are in most cases *inter vivos*. This being the case, they often cause problems of apportionment or identification of the unit of taxation; whether income should be taxed in the hands of a settlor[10] or a beneficiary thereunder. Sections 29 and 30 provide the rules for identifying the person chargeable to tax on income arising in a settlement.

As a general rule, where under any settlement, any income is paid in any year of income during the life of the settlor to or for the benefit of a child of the settlor, such income is deemed to be income of the settlor[320] unless the income so paid does not exceed one hundred shillings or the child attains the age of eighteen years. Note however, only income originating from that settlor shall be taken into account as income paid under the settlement to, or for, the benefit of a child of the settlor. Such income shall be deemed to be the highest part of the settlor's incomes. The basis of liability to tax on income deemed to be income of the settlor is that the law under section 29 (8) deems the settlor to be a person beneficially entitled under the settlement.

Provisions Relating to Revocable Settlements

A settlement is revocable settlement if under its terms the settlor:

a) Has a right to reassume control, directly or indirectly, over the whole or any part of the income arising under the settlement or the assets comprised therein; or

b) Is able to have access, by borrowing or otherwise, to the whole or any part of the income arising under the settlement or the assets comprised therein; or

c) Has power whether immediately or in the future and whether with or without the consent of any other person, to revoke or otherwise determine the settlement and in the event of the exercise of such power, the settlor or the wife or husband of the settlor will or may become beneficially entitled to the whole or any part of the property comprised in the settlement or to the income from the whole or any part of such property.[321]

---

[320] See sections 29 & 30

[321] Su-section 30 (4)

If however, the beneficiary predeceases the settlor, the reasons stated in (a) above shall not render a settlement to be a revocable settlement.[322]

The general rule governing revocable settlements is that all income which in any year of income accrued to or was received by any person under a revocable settlement shall be deemed to be income of the settlor for such year of income and not income of any other person.[323]

If the settlor or his relative or a person under his control either directly or indirectly makes use of any income arising or any accumulated income which has arisen under the settlement, such appropriation shall be deemed to be income of the settlor.[324]

The tax is exacted on the settlor in respect of income arising under a settlement. But, having met the tax liability imposed thereon, the settlor is by law entitled to recover from any trustee or other person to whom the income is payable under the settlement the amount of tax he has paid in respect thereof. And, in this regard the settlor can require the Commissioner to furnish him a certificate specifying the amount of tax he has paid on such income and such certificate shall be conclusive evidence of the facts stated therein.[325]

Clubs and Trade Associations

A "members' club" is defined under sub-section 21 (3) as a club or similar institution all the assets of which are owned by or held in trust for the members thereof. A "trade association" on the other hand, is defined under sub-section 2 (1) as any body of persons which is an association of persons separately engaged in any business with the main object of safeguarding or promoting the business interests of such persons.

Liability of a Members' Club

In principle a members' club can only be liable to tax on the income which they derive from non-members. This is because of the principle

[322] See proviso to sub-section 30 (4)

[323] Sub-section 30 (1)

[324] Sub-section 30 (3)

[325] Sub-section 30 (6)

that a person cannot make a profit from himself.[19] As held in the case of **Carlisle & Silloth Golf Club v. Smith,**[326] profits which derive solely from the suns paid in by members, and belongs to the members on the mutuality principle, would not be taxable. Receipts from non-members are outside the mutuality principle and therefore taxable.

However, sub-section 21 (1) of the Act invades this principle somewhat artificially by deeming the whole of the gross receipts on revenue account, including receipts that would otherwise not be taxable, such as members entrance fees and subscriptions to be income from business.

The charging provision is nevertheless, somehow, mitigated in its effects by a proviso thereto which provides that if three-quarters or more of such receipts are received from members of such club, they will not be deemed to be carrying on a business and such gross receipts shall not be income for tax purposes. In practice however it has proved difficult for the Member's Clubs to keep separate accounts for its members and another for non-members in order to determines whether such club carries on business and hence earn income for the purposes of taxation or otherwise. Conventionally, it appears the tax authorities have been exercising lenience in dealing with such clubs, most of which end up paying little or no tax at all.

Liability of Trade Associations

Traditionally, the mutuality principle extends to trade associations. But, under sub-section 21 (2) a trade association may, in any year of income, by notice in writing to the Commissioner, elect to be deemed to carry on a business charged to tax, whereupon its gross receipts on revenue account from transactions with its members (including entrance fees and annual subscriptions) and with other persons shall be deemed to be income from business.

Cooperative Societies

The taxation of Co-operative Societies is somehow hazy. Paragraph 21 of the First Schedule to the Act exempts the income of primary co-

---

[326] (1913) 3 KB 75

operative societies engaged in three types of activities as follows:

i) Agricultural activities, including activities related to marketing and distribution;

ii) Activities related to the construction of houses for its members; and;

iii) Distribution trade for the benefit of its members.

The Act, however, does not provide for the modality of treating secondary co-operative societies or the apex organisation thereof. Further, it is silent on the treatment of operating surplus of co-operative societies which is distributed to members thereof. Formerly, a tax was levied under section 38 on operating surplus paid to members but this provision was repealed by the Finance Act 1978.

Corporations

It is a fundamental concept of company law that a company is a legal entity distinct from its shareholders, and company law textbooks concentrate on the rights and obligations of a company as an independent legal person. However, the starting point to an understanding of company taxation is economics, not law. Although taxes may be imposed on, and paid by, legal entities such as companies, tax is ultimately borne by individuals. Concentration on corporation tax as solely a tax on companies without considering its implications for shareholders and others will result in a misleading overall picture.

For example, assume a tax system which has no corporation tax and a company which makes profits of Tshs. 100,000/=. Subsequently, tax is introduced at the rate of 50%. One of the effects of the new tax is to reduce from Tshs. 100,000/= to Tshs. 50,000/= the funds available for distribution to shareholders or, if the company retains rather than distributes its profits to reduce the increase in the market value of the shares which would otherwise have occurred. On the other hand, not only shareholders suffer from imposition of corporation tax or alteration of the rates of tax. It is also commercially prudent for companies to pass on the burden of corporation tax in a number of ways. Foremost:

a) It may increase its prices to customers in an attempt to maintain its post-tax profits at pre-tax levels;

b) It may reduce or restrain an increase in the prices it is prepared to pay to its suppliers for goods or services; and

c) It may reduce or restrain the wages it is prepared to pay to its employees.

PRINCIPAL SYSTEMS OF CORPORATE TAXATION

There are three major approaches in taxing corporations.

The Classical System

This is a system where profits of the company are subjected to corporation tax and distributed profits are chargeable to personal income tax. The justification of this system is said to be that a company is a legal person and that the additional tax burden is justifiable because a number of small investors have obtained advantage of combining together to form a mere powerful unit. Further, taxing corporate distributions also encourages capitalisation of profits leading to growth of economy.[327]

It is argued that the tax burden on corporations can be avoided if the company raised its capital from loans (i.e. debt financing) rather than share subscriptions (equity financing) because interest payable on loans is deductible from gross profits of the company. The loan can be invited from the shareholders who may charge interest rates which are higher than the commercial rates.

The Imputation System

Under this system company profits are subjected to corporation tax but when the profits are distributed by way of a dividend part of the

[327] The validity of this is questionable in Tanzania with the existence of section 28 of the Act.

corporation tax paid by the company is treated as tax paid by the shareholders i.e. the tax is imputed to the shareholder as a credit against liability to personal income tax on the distribution.

The Two Rate (Split) System

This system involves the application of two rates upon company profits. A lower rate for distributed profits and a higher rate for undistributed profits.

Taxation of Corporations in Tanzania

There is no separate corporation tax in Tanzania. Corporations are taxed under the Act on the modalities of business income. A corporation which is carrying on business is liable to income tax on its gains or profits from business, or to a capital gains tax on any gains realised from a chargeable disposition of a chargeable asset.

A "corporation" for the purposes of taxation is defined under sub-section 2 (1) of the Act to mean any company or other body. Corporate established, incorporated or registered by or under any law in force in Tanzania.

The Taxation of Corporate Profits

Gains or profits made by a corporation are taxed in the same manner gains or profits from a business or capital gains are taxed. Corporations therefore are subject to the application of sub-section 3 (2) of the Act. As well ascertainment of income chargeable to tax is done in the same manner as if the corporation is a sole trader or a partnership carrying on business. Therefore, all the rules discussed in chapter three in relation to the taxation of business income or income from property, and in chapter four, in relation to capital gains apply to corporations as well, save for an insurance corporations which have special rules as discussed hereunder.

Ascertainment of Income of Insurance Corporations

Section 20 provides the rules of computing the gains or profits of insurance corporations from insurance business which is chargeable to tax. For the purposes of ascertaining gains or profits of an insurance corporation the Act, in sub-section 20 (2), distinguishes between life insurance and insurance business of any other class. It provides that the life insurance business of the corporation shall be treated as a separate business from any other class of insurance business carried on by the corporation. Further, the Act lays down separate rules for the computation of gains or profits from insurance for resident insurance corporations and non-resident insurance corporations.

a) **Resident Insurance Corporations**

The rules for computing gains or profits from insurance business differ as follows:

Insurance Business Other than Life Insurance Business

Regardless of whether the business is of mutual insurance or proprietary insurance, the gains or profits of the resident insurance corporation shall comprise, the amount of the gross premiums for such business, plus the amount of other income from such business including any commission or expense allowance received or receivable from re-insurers and any income derived from investments held in connection with such business. However, premiums returned to the insured and premiums held in connection with such business do not constitute gains and profits from such business.

Several deductions are allowed in ascertaining the gains or profits as follows:

1) A reserve for unexpired risks referable to such business at the percentage adopted by the corporation at the end of the year of income;
2) The amount of claims admitted in such year of income net of any amount recovered in respect thereof under reinsurance;
3) The amount of agency expenses incurred in such year of income in connection with such business;
4) Allowable business expenses.[328]

[328] Sub-section 20 (3)

Life Insurance Business

Where the resident insurance corporation carries on life insurance business, gains or profits therefrom shall be computed separately as follows:

First, the gains or profits shall comprise the difference between the amount of the investment income of its life insurance fund and the expenses of management (including commission). Added thereto, shall be, the amount of any interest paid by such corporation from its annuity fund[329] on surrender of policies or on the return of premiums, other than any such interest which relates to premiums paid under an approved pension scheme or an approved pension fund.[330]

b) **Non-Resident Insurance Corporations**

The same two categorisations as above apply.

Insurance Business Other than Life Insurance Business

The gains or profits of a non-resident insurance corporation from insurance business other than life insurance business is the aggregate of:

1. The amount received or receivable in Tanzania of the gross premiums from such business, excluding premiums returned to the insured and such premiums paid on reinsurance as relates to such business; and
2. The amount of other income from such business, not being income from investments received or receivable in Tanzania, including any commission or expense allowance received or receivable from reinsurance of risk accepted in Tanzania; and
3. The amount of income from investments as the Commissioner may determine to be just and reasonable as representing income from investment of the reserves referable to such business done in Tanzania.[331]

---

[329] Sub-section 20 (5) (a)

[330] Sub-section 20 (5) (b)

[331] Sub-section 20 (4) (a)

Deductions allowed in computing gains or profits therefrom are as follows:

1) A reserve for unexpired risks outstanding at the end of such year of income in respect of policies for which the premiums adopted by the corporation in relation to its insurance business as a whole other than life insurance, plus the reserve for similar unexpired risks at the previous year of income.

2) The amount of claims admitted in such year of income in connection with such business net of the amount recovered in respect thereof under reinsurance.

3) The amount of agency expenses incurred in such year of income in connection with such business.

4) An amount, being such proportion as the Commissioner may determine to be just and reasonable of such of the expenses of the head office of the corporation as would have been allowable as a deduction in such year of income in computing its gains or profits if the corporation had been a resident corporation.[332]

Note, however, that the amounts stated above must relate to policies the premiums of which are received or receivable in Tanzania.[333]

Life Insurance Business

A non-resident insurance corporation carrying on the business of life insurance shall have its gains or profits from such business determined as follows:

First, there shall be included, the same proportion of the investment income of its life insurance fund as the life insurance premiums received in Tanzania bear to the total life insurance premiums received or, if the Commissioner so determines it to be just and reasonable, as the actuarial liability in respect of its life insurance business (other than its annuity business) in Tanzania bears to the actuarial liability in respect of its total life insurance business (other than its annuity business).[334]

---

[332] Sub-section 20 (4) (b) and (c)

[333] Sub-section 20 (4) (c)

[334] Sub-section 20 (6) (a)

Second, there shall be deducted from the amount ascertained in the first step above, the life insurance expenses of agencies in Tanzania and such proportion as the Commissioner may determine to be just and reasonable of such of the life insurance expenses of the head office of such corporation as would have been allowable as a deduction in such year of income in computing its gains or profits if the corporation had been a resident corporation.[335]

Third, there shall be included to the net amount as ascertained in the foregoing first and second steps, the amount of any interest paid by such corporation from its annuity fund on the surrender of policies the premiums in respect of which were received in Tanzania or on the return of premiums received in Tanzania other than any such interest which relates to premiums paid under an approved pension scheme or an approved pension fund.[336]

THE TAXATION OF CORPORATE DISTRIBUTIONS

Corporate distributions include ordinary dividends, dividend in kind and stock dividends, deemed dividends, shareholder benefits and inter-corporate dividends.

Ordinary Dividends

The term "dividend" is not defined by the Act, therefore, it must be given its ordinary meaning for corporate law purposes. In the case of **Hill v. Permanent Trustee Company of New South Wales Ltd**[337] the following statement was made:

> A limited company not in liquidation can make no payment by way of return of capital to its shareholders except as a step in an authorised reduction of capital. Any other payment made by it by means of which it parts with moneys to its shareholders must and can only be made by way of dividing profits. Whether the payment is called "dividend" or "bonus" or any other name, it still must remains a payment on a division of profits.

[335] Sub-section 20 (6) (b)

[336] Sub-section 20 (6) (c)

[337] [1930]AC 720

Thus any distribution by a corporation of its income or capital gains made pro rata among its shareholders many properly be described as a dividend, unless the corporation can show that it is another type of payment. Such amounts payable to shareholders by a company are income chargeable to tax under sub-section 3 (2) (b) of the Act and it is taxable in the year of income in which it is paid. However, one must note the restrictive language used in sub-section 7 (1) (a), that is, only a dividend paid by a resident corporation is chargeable to tax as income.

Dividends in Kind and Stock Dividends

If a corporation distributes assets by way of a dividend, the shareholders are in receipt of a dividend in the amount of the fair market value of such assets. The distributing corporation is considered to have disposed of the property for its fair market value. This is dividend in kind. A stock dividend on the other hand is a dividend paid by a corporation by the issuance of any shares of the corporation, for example, in Tanzania, the issuance of bonus shares, under the Companies Ordinance,[338] from the capital redemption fund or issuance of preference shares at a discount.

Under sub-section 7 (1) (c) such dividends are taxable only if they take the form of issuance of debentures or redeemable preference shares to shareholders at a discount of more than five percent of their nominal value or redeemable value.[339]

Deemed Dividends

These only relate to private companies, in respect of which the Commissioner has power, if he is of the opinion that, such a private company has not distributed a dividend within a reasonable period, to deem a portion of the income of such company as a dividend declared and distributed to shareholders.[340] Section 28 imposes some restriction on the Commissioner in the exercise of such power.

---

338 Sub-section 47 (1) (c) and (4) of Cap. 212

339 See the *proviso* to sub-section 7 (10 (c) and the provisions of paragraph (d) thereof relating to branch dividend

340 Section 28 of the Act

First, the reasonable period referred to above shall be a period not exceeding twelve months after the end of the private company's accounting period.

Second, the amount deemed must be such part of the private company's income for that period as could lawfully be so distributed without prejudice to the requirements of the company's business. In this regard, the Commissioner was required observe the relevant regulations in the **Companies (Regulation of Dividend, Surpluses and Miscellaneous Provisions) Act**. 1972[341] which laid down the rules for determination of the declarable dividend. However, with the repeal of the said Act, the law is now unclear on how the determination should be guided. Probably the Commissioner will maintain departmental practice shaped through the application of the repealed legislation.

The dividend deemed to be distributed shall be deemed to have been paid on a date twelve months after the end of the company's accounting period.

Shareholders Benefits

Shareholder benefits take various focus. For example, in the case of **Guilder News Co. v. MNR**[342] it took the form of the sale of corporate property to the shareholder for an amount less than the fair market value of the property. In the case of **Losey v. MNR**[343] the benefit accrued to the shareholder in a sale of property of the shareholder to the corporation for an amount in excess of the fair market value of the property. In **Byke v. The Queen**[344] the benefit was the payment by a corporation of a shareholder's personal expenses. Other benefits to shareholders include the rent-free use of corporate property by a shareholder and interest-free or low-interest loans to shareholders.

---

[341] Act No. 22 of 1972

[342] [1973]CTC 1; 73 DTC 5048 (F.C.A.)

[343] [1957] CTC 146; 57 DTC 1098

[344] [1974] CTC 763; 74 DTC 6585

Although there is no express provision in the Act as to the taxability of shareholder benefits as dividend income still the same can be taxable under sub-section 3 (2) (b) on the basis of the judicial definition of the term dividend as pointed in the case of **Hill v. Permanent Trustee Company of New South Wales, Ltd** (*supra*). However, this is subject to the judicial authorities in Tanzania adopting the said interpretation.

Inter-Corporate Dividends

These are dividends paid by one corporation to another. For example, most government owned holding corporations such as the National Development Corporation, the National Textile Corporation and the like earn a greater percentage of their income from dividends payable to them by their subsidiaries. Such dividend is deemed to be not income if received by a resident corporation where such corporation controls directly or indirectly twenty five or more percent of the voting power of the corporation paying the dividend.[345]

Corporate Distributions on Winding-Up

Sub-section 7 (1) (b) provides that, when, in relation to any corporation that is being wound up voluntarily, any profits whether earned before or during the winding up are distributed (whether in cash or otherwise) the distribution shall be deemed to be a payment of dividend and thus taxable under sub-section 3 (2) (b).

The Rates of Tax

Sub-section 33 (1) (d) provides for the corporation rate of tax. The rates, however, are contained in Paragraph 5 in the Third Schedule which are subject to variations by the annual Finance Acts. A different rate applies to dividend income in Paragraph 5 (a) in the Third Schedule.[346]

---

[345] See *proviso* to sub-section 7 (2)

[346] See also Third schedule No 2

Problems in Taxing Corporations

1) Corporation tax is imposed by reference to accounting periods. In other tax jurisdictions a problem has arisen on how to treat corporation accounting periods straddling two financial or calendar years. In Tanzania, section 31 provides that where a taxpayer's accounting period overlaps a calendar year, the taxpayer's year of income shall be the year in which the accounting period ends. The tax is levied on a "preceding year basis," for example, a corporation files its return of income for the preceding year in January the following year. This should be distinguished from individuals who pay tax on a "current year basis."

2) As noted in the introductory part on the topic of taxation of corporations, it is still debatable whether the corporation or the shareholder should suffer tax. The main argument is that the tax paid by the corporation is actually borne by the shareholder in the form of reduced profits available for distribution as dividends.

3) The classical system used in Tanzania distorts neutrality in the tax system. Ideally, the total tax paid by the corporation and the shareholder should not exceed or be less than the total tax paid by an individual hence the arguments for integration. Lack of a dividend tax credit in the Act perpetuates the inequities arising from the system, in particular the double taxation of corporate profits.

4) It is common for an organisation with a number of different businesses to use separate companies for each business. For company law purposes, each company is a legal entity distinct from other companies in the group, but this legal demarcation could have considerable disadvantages from a tax view point, with, for example, losses in one company not being available for deduction from profits of another company in the group. In other countries, for example, UK. the tax legislation contains provisions which enable a group of companies to be taxed as if they were one entity although problems have arisen regarding the definition of a group and inexhaustiveness of the provisions

dealing with inter-group transactions. The Income Tax Act, 1973 is silent on this issue.

5) Treatment of close corporations. The tax legislation must ensure that conducting business through, or holding investments in a small family company does not confer significant tax advantage on the shareholder ultimately beneficially entitled to the company's profits. For example, an individual can create a company to receive all income from the investments thus attracting the favourable corporation tax rate and use the company to retain profits (undistributed profits) hence deferring almost indefinitely his individual tax liability. Although section 28 of the Act is intended to curb this practice it is not adequate in the complex business environment of today.

A company is a close company if either:

a) It is controlled by its directors;

b) Controlled by a related group of persons; or

c) Controlled by very few participators who are entitled to the majority of share capital, or a majority of the distributable income.

A "participator" include a shareholder and a loan creditor. Ideally, in counting the shares or interests of a participator, there has to be included any share or interests in the company owned by the participator's "associates," namely, his spouse, parents, grandparents, children, brothers, sisters, partners, trustees of related trusts, generally all those who do not deal at arm's length. No double counting should be permitted, so that a wife's shares must either be counted as her own or her husband's, but if any combination results if fewer people having control, the company is close. The Act again does not address this problem.

10

INTERNATIONAL TAXATION

INTRODUCTION

As national tax systems become highly developed and rooted in nationally conceived principles, levels of taxation rose and international economic relationships became more complex and the problems arising from multinational claims to tax revenue became more pressing.

In principle a sovereign country enjoys unrestricted powers to design and implement taxes. However, a government's fiscal claim would remain thereoretical if the physical possibility to reach the taxable object and, or the tax subject were lacking. Thus, although there are no rules of international law to limit the extent of any country's tax jurisdiction, a country generally does not impose a tax unless the business transaction or its participants have a significant connection with the country. Thus, for example, Tanzania is unable to tax a Kenyan corporation, owned by a Sudanese citizen living in Uganda, that sells Japanese made goods located in Taiwan to a Zambian corporation owned by a British resident, when the sale documents are signed in Zimbabwe, payment in US dollars made in Belgium, and the goods are to be shipped to Burundi and ultimately used in Zaire. Of course one or more of these other countries may be able to impose a tax on the profit, if any, from this endeavour.

JURISDICTION TO IMPOSE TAX

There are two basic kinds of jurisdictional connection:

Personal Jurisdiction

Generally, countries which tax income only at the recipient's domicile or residence follow the global system of taxation i.e. all income from whatever source derived, that accrue to the same taxpayer, are taxed together as a single mass of income. Most Anglophone countries follow this system. Under the global system the jurisdictional connection is the personal status of the taxpayer. The global system taxes the world-wide income of a taxpayer regardless of its geographical source.

Source Jurisdiction

Under the source jurisdiction, a state taxes all income earned from sources within its territorial jurisdiction. This principle is generally used in countries with a schedular. System, for example, most Franco-phone countries, Latin America, Belgium and Italy. The essence of the system is the concept that there are qualitative differences in different kinds of income. Thus each different kind is taxed under different rules and at different rates. The jurisdictional connection is the source of income, not the personal status of the taxpayer, and only income from what are considered to be domestic sources is taxed, such as, property situated in the country, or income derived therefrom, income produced by an activity (employment on business) carried on the country, and transactions carried out in the country, for example, the sales of goods, the transfer of property, etecetra.

Note, however, most countries today apply a combination of these two jurisdictional principles. For example, a country which taxes its citizens or residents on their world income and also taxes income derived by non-residents from sources within its territorial jurisdiction.

HOW DOUBLE TAXATION ARISES

The concurrent application of tax systems based in varying degrees on the source, residence and citizenship principles inevitably give rise to overlapping assertions of tax jurisdictions, resulting in international double taxation in the following ways:

Dual Residence

Two countries may treat a person (individual or company) a resident in its country and tax him on his world-wide income or capital because of his personal link with the two countries.

The dual residence form of double taxation arises when countries use different tests to determine the fiscal home of their taxpayers. For example, with respect to individuals, country A may claim residence jurisdiction over a taxpayer who is domiciled within its territory, but who spent most of his tax year working in country B, while country B asserts residence jurisdiction over the same taxpayer because he has net the limited stay test of residence which country B employs A corporation may also be subject to dual residence double taxation if it is organised in one country which uses a place of incorporation test to determine residence jurisdiction, and managed in another country which uses a place-of-effective management test as its residence criterion.

Source Conflicts

Two countries may assert tax jurisdiction over a transaction. Each claiming that income (under its source of income rules) was generated within its borders and thus is subject to its taxing powers. Rules for determining the territorial source of various types of income are very fluid in their application by different jurisdictions. Assuming that the jurisdictions even purport to apply the same rules, may yield different results. This leads to source conflicts between countries. One kind of source conflict relates to the source of income derived from services rendered by construction and engineering firms in country A undertaking projects in other countries with tax systems quite different from country A's. The services for which these firms are paid are usually carried out both in country A (design, research etc.) and in the other countries (e.g. supervision). Country A may view that in such cases, only that portion of the income which directly relates to the actual activities performed outside of country A may be regarded as having a foreign source and tax the income of home-source. The other countries, however, will often impose an income tax on the entire contract profit.

Another kind of source conflict occurs when an enterprise in country A has a permanent establishment in country B which derives income from country C and the income is concurrently taxed in countries B and C.

A third source conflict arising where both the lending country and the borrowing country claim that its country's the source-country of the interest and asserts tax jurisdiction on the same interest arisen from the transaction.

There is still another source conflict which arises where one foreign jurisdiction imposes a non-resident withholding tax similar to the have country version, but the income cannot be properly treated as having its source in that jurisdiction. In this situation, the tax paid in the foreign country cannot be deducted if the home country adopts the foreign tax credit system.

Residence-Source Double Taxation

This is a situation where one country taxes a person on his world-wide income or capital because he is resident there, and the other country taxes the same person on income he derives from that country or on capital situated therein, hence, the conflict of residence against source.

Residence - source double taxation can arise despite the absence of definitional problems concerning the residence of the taxpayer or the source of the income. This form of double taxation will occur any time country A taxes its residents on their world-wide income and a resident of that country derives income from a source within country B, a country that taxes that income at source.

METHODS OF ELIMINATING OF DOUBLE TAXATION

Although there are no principles of international law or even constitutional law which require relief to be given for double taxation, this fact does not mean that relief is generally denied. The necessities of commercial and fiscal co-existence, the considerations of administrative convenience, and the requirement of equitable treatment between investors at home and abroad, have led the nations of the world voluntarily to limit the scope of their tax jurisdictions. Some of the restrictions are unilateral, some are bilateral and some even become multilateral.

Unilateral Relief From Double Taxation

Since the rise in income tax rates that followed World War I, unilateral relief has become fairly common. Most countries now have some provisions in their internal tax law to take account of the tax liabilities borne, or presumably borne, by their taxpayers in the countries in which their foreign source income originated. Unilateral methods of relief generally fall into one of the following categories:

Exemption

A number of countries adopt an exemption system as a unilateral measure for the avoidance of double taxation. This could either be fully or in part i.e. by excluding certain types of foreign source income in computing taxable income of their residents. The exemption method is often used with regard to business profits from permanent establishments and dividends from direct investment. The exemption method is designed to achieve capital import neutrality as regards the exempted items of income, i.e. the taxpayer is placed in a position of tax equality with the residents of the source country because the foreign taxpayer pays the same income tax as the local taxpayer. Although it may lead to a source of income escaping tax completely and despite the fact that no government likes to absolutely relinquish its right to tax income. This method is widely used by Western European countries. The exemption system is in two major forms.

a) *Full Exemption*

Whereby the foreign source income is not taken into account at all in the investor's home country. Countries which offer such exemption include Argentina, Austria, Australia, Brazil, the Netherlands, Switzerland and France.

b) *Exemption with Progression*

Whereby the income which may be taxed in the source country is not taxed in the residence country, but the country of residence reserves the

the right to take the exempted income into account in determining the tax rate to be applied to the balance of income of the taxpayer, so that it may in practice, constitute a partial tax on the otherwise exempted income.

For example, a taxpayer has shs. 80,000/= income in country R, shs. 20,000/= in country S, and if the tax rate in country R is 35% on shs. 100,000/= and 30% on Shs. 80,000/= then he will be taxed in country R in three different ways according to the unilateral method applied by that country as follows:

i) No relief: thus, his total amount of tax is Shs. 35,000/= (i.e. 100,000/= x 35%).

ii) Full exemption: thus, his total amount of tax is Shs. 24,000/= (80,000/= x 30%). Only his shs. 80,000/= income in country R is taxed. He gets a relief of shs. 11,000/= (35,000 - 24,000).

iii) Exemption with progression: thus, his total amount of tax is shs. 28,000/= (80,000 x 30%). Country R imposes tax on Shs. 80,000/= at the 35% rate of tax applicable to total income (100,000/=). He gets a relief of shs. 7,000/= (35,000 - 28,000). Countries which have used this method of unilateral relief include Belgium, Norway and Portugal.

Tax Credit

The essential feature of the credit method is that the investor's country of residence treats the foreign tax, within certain statutory limitations, as if it were a tax deemed to be paid to itself. Where the foreign tax rate is lower than the domestic rate only the excess of the domestic tax over the foreign tax is payable to the residence country. Where the foreign tax is the higher one, the country of residence does not collect any tax. The effective overall tax burden is determined by the higher of the domestic or the foreign tax rate. The foreign tax credit system is applied by, and was developed in, the domestic law of Anglo-American countries. The US was the first to utilize the tax credit on a world wide basis. In Canada it was introduced in 1949 and in the UK. in 1916 but applied only to income from within the Dominions and colonies.

This method is used to achieve capital export neutrality since the recipient of foreign source income receives the same tax treatment as taxpayers with only domestic source income. Direct foreign tax credit may be applied in two main ways:

First, the residence country allows the deduction of the total amount of tax paid in the other country on income which may be taxed in that country, hence, full credit.

Second, the deduction given by the residence country for the tax paid in the other country is restricted to that part of its own tax appropriate to the income which may be taxed in the other country. This is ordinary credit applied in Canada, Colombia, Denmark, Germany, Finland, Japan, Spain, Sweden, the UK and the USA.

An indirect tax credit system is adopted in a number of countries, under which domestic corporations can deem as paid by themselves the portion of foreign corporation tax paid by their subsidiaries corresponding to the dividends they receive, and credit it against their domestic income tax e.g. in Canada, Denmark, Germany, Japan, the UK and USA.

There are some limitations upon the effectiveness of foreign tax credit systems. The primary limitation is the delineation of taxes in respect of which relief is offered.

Tax Deduction

This approach consists of allowing the deduction of taxes already paid in the host country not against the home country tax (as in the foreign tax credit) but against the (world-wide) taxable base in the country of residence. The taxes due abroad are viewed as costs of doing business and as a deduction in computing taxable income.

Bilateral Relief from Double Taxation

Even though various countries employ various unilateral measures to cope with the problem of international double taxation, virtually all industrialised countries have found it necessary to supplement these measures by entering into a network of tax treaties with their principal commercial partners and other countries with which their taxpayers are involved in trade or investment. This is mainly because the functions of unilateral relief are limited, and there are still many barriers and instances of double taxation which make international trade and investment difficult. Tax treaties are bilateral agreements or conventions negotiated between countries for the purpose of resolving double taxation problems which arise from the assertion by more than one country, through internal laws, of jurisdiction to tax the same item of income.

This form of relief entails an agreement between countries in which each country agrees to modify its own tax laws to achieve reciprocal benefits. It can usually eliminate or reduce double taxation through an exclusion from taxation, a special rate on certain types of income and provisions for "competent" authority procedures to redress cases of double taxation. Tax treaties also encourage discussions at government levels with respect to tax systems. Further tax authorities gain a lot under such treaties because they acquire substantially greater access to information concerning the activities of taxpayers.

Bilateral relief may either take the form of tax exemption or a tax credit. It may involve the exemption method whereby tax jurisdiction over specified categories of income is assigned exclusively to one of the contracting parties, and the other agrees to exempt that category of income from tax, or refrain from exercising its jurisdiction to tax the particular income in question.

One needs to note the problems of using the tax credit method by developing countries in trying to attract foreign investments. Most of such incentives accrue not to the foreign investors but to their countries of residence. In order to make sure that the investors benefit and not the home country government, many developing countries insist on having a "tax sparring" clause in the tax treaties with developed countries.

A typical tax treaty is designed to deal with three forms of double taxation. The dual residence problem with respect to individuals is resolved by a series of rules establishing a hierarchy among the various tests of residence. To solve the source conflict double taxation problem, contracting states can provide common source of income rules in tax conventions. For example, the provision in the OECD model state that the following classes of income and capital are taxed without any limitation in the state of source:

a) Income from immovable property situated in that state (including income from agriculture or forestry) and gains from alienation of such property (see Article 6 thereof).

b) Profits of a permanent establishment situated in that state (Article 7).

c) The directors' fees paid by a company which is a resident of that state (Article 16) etc.

There are three ways in which tax treaties can handle the residence - source double taxation. First, the treaty might assign exclusive jurisdiction to tax to the country of residence thereby relieving the country of source of its authority to tax.

For example, in the OECD Model Treaty, royalty payments (Article 12) and payments received by a student for the purpose of his/her education or training (Article 20), profits from the operation of ships or aircraft in international traffic or of boats, gains from alienation of such ships, boats or aircraft and capital represented by them, are taxable only in the state in which the place of effective management of the enterprise is situated.

Second, the treaty might assign the right to tax exclusively to the source country eliminating double taxation by taking away the jurisdiction of the residence country. For example, Article 19 of the OECD model on pension payment.

Third, concurrent residence and source may be retained, but the country of residence must give relief to the extent to which the source country asserts its right to tax as in the case of dividend and interest. Note that in such cases the rate of tax applied by the source country is usually also limited.

Multilateral Relief from Double Taxation

Such reliefs are relatively uncommon. There are very few so far. The Multinational Tax Treaty for central Europe signed by Austria, Hungary, Poland, Italy, Romania and Yugoslavia was the first to be signed in 1922, but only two countries ratified it and thus it because a bilateral one.[10]

The most comprehensive multilateral double taxation convention was concluded in 1983 among Nordic countries. Others include the OCAM Treaty of 1971 (L'organisation Commune Africaine, Malagache et Mauricienne) between Cameroon, CAR, Chad, Congo, Dahoney, Ivory Coast, Malagasy, Mauritius, Niger, Rwanda, Senegal, Togo, Upper Volta and Zaire. The Audean Tax Treaty of 1972 by Bolivia, Chile, Colombia, Equador and Peru, - however, Chile subsequently denounced the treaty; and the Arab Tax Treaty of 1973. Only the Adean Treaty is effective (as from 1/1/1981). Among the CMEA (comecon) countries, two multilateral tax conventions have been in force since 1979 and there is also a single income class multilateral convention i.e. the UNESCO-WIPO convention on the avoidance of double taxation of copyright royalties of 1979.

Multilateral tax treaties are usually entered into by countries with some special historical, cultural or economic relationship, such as, the Nordic countries; or similarity in their tax systems, such as, the CMEA countries. Bilateral treaties still exist between countries with multilateral treaties. Multilateral treaties may have advantage of more uniformity in regulations and interpretation. They also promote co-operation among contracting states. Like bilateral tax treaties, multilateral conventions may apply the methods of exemption, credit or deduction to eliminate double taxation.

Multilateral conventions are rare due to large variations among domestic tax systems. A major disadvantage of it is its rigidity.

Other Functions of Tax Treaties

Originally and primarily tax treaties are used to eliminate double taxation. But they also serve a number of other important functions. First, they help to prevent tax avoidance and tax evasion by including provisions for mutual agreement procedure and exchange of information.

Second, they help to allocate tax revenue generated by international investment between contracting states. Third, they reduce tax harassment.

Fourth, they create certainty and predictability regarding international investment.

Fifth, they provide an improvement in the general business atmosphere by offering reassurance to investors and businessmen that there exists a mechanism for the settlement of tax grievances that may arise.

Sixth, they form a bridge between different tax systems so as to reduce frictions and distortions existing between them, for example, between developing and developed countries; between socialist and capitalist countries.

AN OVERVIEW OF MODEL TAX CONVENTIONS

The international efforts to deal with the problems of international double taxation were begun by the League of Nations and have been pursued in the Organisation for Economic Co-operation and Development (OECD) and regional for, as well as in the United Nations, have in general found concrete expression in a series of model bilateral tax conventions.

Draft model conventions include the 1927 model treaty, 1928 model conventions, the 1935 draft convention, the 1943 Mexico model, the 1946 London model, name of which gained widespread acceptance. In 1967 the OECD drafted a model convention which was later revised in 1977.

The OECD Model

This rests on two fundamental premises:

1) The country of residence eliminates double taxation by giving a credit or exemption.
2) The source country in turn, reduce considerably the scope of its jurisdiction to tax at source, and reduce the rate of tax where jurisdiction is retained.

This model has been followed in tax treaties made between developed countries. Developing countries have in their tax treaties with developed countries usually accepted the first premise, that is, they agree that the residence country, usually the developed country, should give a credit or exemption to eliminate double taxation. But have frequently rejected the second premise.

Note that, income flows between developed countries in a two way traffic, thus it makes little difference to them whether their tax treaties emphasise source or residence jurisdiction. In contrast, between developed and developing countries, income flows in a one way traffic so that the developing countries should not be expected to sacrifice their national revenue and foreign exchange reserves.

The UN Model

This attempts to strike a compromise between the source principle and the residence principle by giving more weight to the source principle than does the OECD model. To mitigate this source bias the UN model embodies the premise that the source country recognises that:

a) Taxation of income from capital be done on a net basis, i.e. taking into account expenses allocable to the earnings of income.

b) Taxation would not be so high as to discourage investment.

c) It may be appropriate for a country to share revenue with the country providing the capital.

Besides the above world-wide model bilateral conventions, there are a number of regional and sub-regional conventions, for example, the 1976 LAFTA Convention (i.e. Latin American Free Trade Association), the 1971 model convention by the commission of the Cartagena Agreement and others by most developed countries, but only the US has published its model treaty.[13]

The US Model 1981

This sets out the official US policy in its negotiations with other countries on new and revised income tax treaties. Note that, like most other countries, the US recorded reservations to the substantive provisions in the OECD model that it considered unacceptable. Thus a principal purpose of the US Model is to align US tax treaty negotiations with both the substance and form of the OECD model to the extent consistent with US tax law and policy. The second purpose is to indicate to those countries with whom the US conduct treaty negotiations those changes and exceptions the US finds necessary in accommodating the OECD model to the US tax structure.

Apparently, the US strongly holds its own positions such as the fundamental rule that the US reserves in treaties the right generally to tax the world-wide income of its citizens and corporations without regard to the treaty. This is known as the "saving clause." For example, under Article 1 of the US Model, a US citizen residing in the other treaty country is not eligible for the lower US treaty rates on dividends and interest from US corporations.

Further, the US jurisprudence does not employ certain concepts found in the OECD model. For instance, the determination of residence of corporations on the basis of the location of effective management. The US insists that the residence of a corporation is the country where it is incorporated. Also the US desires to deal with certain matters, such as partnerships and social security which OECD suggests are more appropriately left to bilateral solutions. The US is also concerned about tax treaty abuses, especially tax havens and secrecy laws of certain tax havens.

THE TANZANIAN APPROACH

Provisions Dealing with International Double Taxation Under the Income Tax Act, 1973

In Tanzania, like other countries the problem of international double taxation exists because of the application of both residence and source principles of tax jurisdiction. Under sub-section 3 (1) (a) & (b) read together with sub-section 2 (2), income tax is levied on resident persons on worldwide income, and non-residents on their Tanzania source income, for example, employment income, withholding tax under sub-section 34(1) in respect of management or professional fee, royalty, rent and any income from property, dividend, interest or pension and retirement annuity. Reliefs provided for under the Act in respect of international double taxation include:

Exemption

This is offered under section 15 of the Act. The Minister of Finance is empowered to exempt any income or class of income accrued in or derived from Tanzania from the income tax. This power has frequently been exercised by the Minister to grant relief to foreign companies and individuals (expatriate staff). The relief of exemption is also possible under a special arrangement as provided for in sub-section 44 (7).

Tax Credit

These are covered under Sections 42, 43 and 44 of the Act. Section 42 allows a tax credit in respect of income tax paid by a resident person in a Partner State, in respect of income accrued in or derived from such Partner State.

Section 43 gives a force of law to bilateral arrangements between the government of Tanzania and any foreign government with a view to affording relief from double taxation or any tax of a similar character imposed by the laws of that place.

Under section 44 foreign tax payable in respect of any income will be allowed as a credit against tax chargeable in respect of such income i.e. the amount of tax chargeable upon such income shall be reduced by the amount of the credit. This credit is only allowed if:

a) There is special arrangement; and

b) The claimant taxpayer is resident in Tanzania in such year of income; and

c) The credit shall not exceed the amount of the tax chargeable upon the income in respect of which the credit is to be allowed[347] ; and

d) Any person may elects by a notice in writing to the Commissioner that such credit shall not be allowed in the case of his income for such year of income[348] .

Section 45 is a limitation provision. It provides that any claim for an allowance by way of credit shall be made to the Commissioner within six years from the end of the year of income to which it relates. In addition, Tanzania has entered into several "tax sparring" treaties to give effect to tax credits, for example, with Denmark, Italy and Sweden.

Reduced Tax Rates

Paragraph 4 (f) in the Third Schedule to the Act provides a special rate of 12.5 percent in respect of pension or retirement annuity payable to a non-resident who is a resident of a country with which the government of Tanzania has arrangement for relief of double taxation. Generally, under paragraph 4 in the Third Schedule, non-residents enjoy relatively lower rates of tax.

---

[347] Sub-section 44 (4)

[348] Sub-section 44 (b)

11

RIGHTS AND OBLIGATIONS OF TAXPAYERS

OBLIGATIONS OF TAXPAYERS

Every taxpayer has an obligation to pay the tax assessed and due in respect of any year of income. Determination of tax payable is effected through assessment procedures which begin with the submission of returns of income to the Commissioner.

Procedure for Submission of Returns

The requirement for submitting returns of income is contained in sub-section 57 (1) which provide that, the Commissioner may by notice in writing require any person to furnish a return of income. Where no such notice is issued by the Commissioner within four months after the end of the year of income, every person with income chargeable to tax has an obligation to give notice in writing to the Commissioner that he is chargeable to tax. The requirement for submitting returns does not, however, apply to three categories of taxpayers, namely:

a) A person who carries on business the accounting period or which ends on some day other than 31st December and has made a return of income for such year of income within four months of the end of such accounting period.

b) An employee if he/she has no income other than income from emoluments, or whose tax has been deducted through the withholding tax under Part IX of the Act.

c) An individual farmer who has elected that his income be ascertained by a District Advisory Committee under sub-section 57 (4).

Types of Returns

Basically there are two types of returns of income, namely: normal returns and provisional returns. However, the Act empowers the Commissioner to require any person to furnish him with returns aimed at gathering information or preventing evasion, these are referred to as occasional returns.

Normal Returns

These are returns furnished after a notice has been issued under sub-section 57 (1). The practice is for the Department of Income Tax to issue forms for normal returns in January following the year of income to which they relate. Normal returns have to be completed by taxpayers and filed with the Commissioner within a reasonable time, not being less than thirty days from the date of service of notice, and in the case of a person carrying on a business who has made a provisional return of income, such normal return (referred to as final return in such cases) may be filed within a period not exceeding six[349] months from the date to which he/she makes up the accounts of such business.

Further, the Commissioner is empowered, under sub-section 57 (2), to issue notice for filing return of income in the case of executors or administrators of a deceased person, or of a liquidator of a resident company or partners of a firm being wound up, or of a bankrupt, or of any person whom he/she has reason to believe is about to leave Tanzania at any time whether before or after the end of the year of income to which such return relates.

---

[349] The Finance Act, 1999 has reduced the number of months to six from the previous nine months

Provisional Returns

These are returns submitted by individuals, firms or companies deriving their income from business. They are provided for under section 58. The Commissioner may require any person other than an employee or a person who has been required to furnish a normal return under sub-section 57 (1) and has furnished the same, to furnish a provisional return.

A provisional return is a kind of self-assessment by the taxpayer. It has to be submitted, in the case of a person other than an individual, not later than 31st March following the year of income to which such return relates, and in the case of an individual not later than 31st March in the year of income to which the return relates.[350]

Unlike in a normal return, in a provisional return the taxpayer shall estimate his income chargeable to tax, the tax chargeable on such income and shall make a declaration that such return contains full and true estimates of his income and tax to the best of his/her knowledge and belief.[351]

A provisional return can be amended by an individual taxpayer by filing an amended provisional return if during the year of income he discovers that the provisional return furnished is likely to be substantially incorrect because of changed circumstances or where he/she is dissatisfied with an estimated provisional assessment raised by the Commissioner under sub-section 80 (3).

Where no notice to file a provisional return has been issued, the taxpayer him/herself must notify the Commissioner that he/she has not received such notice within fourteen days of the expiration of the statutory period for filing provisional return.[352]

Occasional Returns

In order to provide the tax authorities with information to enable them to trace potential taxpayers and prevent evasion of tax, the Act empowers the Commissioner to require any person to furnish returns containing details of payments made to other person and as useful information.

---

[350] Sub-section 58 (2) (a)

[351] Sub-section 58 (2) (c)

[352] Sub-section 58 (3)

For instance:

i) Return by an employer giving details of persons employed and salaries paid to them;[353]

ii) Return by businesses giving details of fees, commissions, royalties etc. paid for services rendered by other persons;[354]

iii) Return by occupiers giving names and addresses of lodgers and tenants and the rents payable by them;[355]

iv) Return on dividends paid by a resident corporation;[356]

v) Return as to interest paid or credited by banks;[357]

vi) Return as to income exempt from tax;[358] and

vii) Return as to income received on account of other persons.[359]

Such returns shall be filed within a reasonable time specified by the Commissioner in the notice, provided that such specified time shall not be less than thirty days from the date of service of such notice. Section 76 empowers the Commissioner to extend the period for filing such return.

Requirements in Respect of Returns

a) ***Declaration***

All returns must contain a declaration signed by the person filing the same that the return is a full and true statement. Sections 117 and 118 imposes sanctions for making incorrect returns, giving false information, making false claims or making fraudulent returns.

b) ***Accounts***

Save for occasional returns, all returns must be accompanied by a copy of the balance sheet and the trading profit and loss account.

---

[353] Section 63
[354] Section 64
[355] Sections 65 and 66
[356] Section 72
[357] Section 73
[358] Section 68
[359] Section 77

c) ***Verification of Accounts***

The copies of the balance sheet or trading profit and loss account must:

i) Be signed by the taxpayer or authorised auditor or authorised accountant.

ii) Be accompanied by a certificate signed by such person. Where the accounts were prepared by an authorised auditor or authorised accountant, the certificate shall specify the nature of books of account and documents from which such accounts were so prepared and shall state to what extent he or she considers the accounts to present a true and fair view of the gains or profits from the business.[360]

d) ***Certain Returns to be Prepared by Authorised Auditor or Accountant***

Section 60 imposes a requirement that a return of income or a provisional return of income must be prepared and certified by an authorised auditor or an authorised accountant[361] within the meaning assigned thereto by the Auditors and Accountants (Registration) Act, 1972 except where the return of income is of an individual or a partnership firm:[362]

i) The whole of whose income is derived from employment, and that such income has been fully subjected to PAYE deductions; and

ii) In the case of a partnership, if its annual gross turnover is less that one million five hundred thousand shillings.[363]

---

360 See full requirements under section 59

361 Subject to section 2 of Act No. 2 of 1995 the terms and definitions of "Authorised Auditor" and "Authorised Accountant" have been deleted and substitute for "Certified Public Accountant in Public Service" and "Certified public Accountant" respectively and definitions thereof.

362 Note the special requirements in sub-section 61 (4) relating to miningy operations

363 According to sub-section 60 (2) (c) the "annual gross turnover" refers to the volume of business transacted by a partnership firm in a year, measured in sales or revenue.

e) ***Records***

Every taxpayer must keep proper books of account and records and preserve the same for a period of not less than 10 years after the year of income to which such books and records relate,[364] and he/she shall at any time produce them for examination or retention by the Commissioner, and shall not destroy, damage or deface them.[365]

Failure to File Returns

Section 78 provides that any person who fails to file a return of income or a provisional return or to give notice to the Commissioner as required in sections 57 and 58 shall for each period of one month or part thereof during which such failure continues, be charged with additional tax equal to 2.5 percent of the normal tax in the case of failure to furnish a normal return and 2 percent of the normal tax in the case of failure to furnish a provisional return. In each case, however, such additional tax shall not be less than five hundred shillings where the defaulter is an individual one thousand shillings for any other case. The Commissioner may, if furnished with reasonable cause. remit the whole or any part of additional tax.[366]

Additional tax may also be imposed where the taxpayer omits from his return of income any amount which should have been included, claims a deduction to which he/she is not entitled or makes any incorrect statement in relation to any matter affecting his/her tax liability, whether due to fraud or gross neglect. The tax to be charged shall be equal to three times the amount omitted or lessened.[367]

Note that the liability for the additional tax due to any such failure, omission, claim, statement, deduction or unwarranted set of extends severally and jointly, in the case of a person filing such return on behalf of another person to both of them, and in the case of a return prepared and certified by an authorised auditor or authorised accountant

[364] Sub-section 61 (2)

[365] Sub-section 62 (1)

[366] See sub-section 78 (1) and the proviso (ii) to sub-section 78 (1) (b)

[367] Sub-section 78 (2)

to such auditor or accountant as well as the person to whom the return relates.[368]

POWERS AND OBLIGATIONS OF THE COMMISSIONER

Notice of Chargeability

As discussed above, the Commissioner, may, under sections 57 and 58 issue notice to taxpayers or persons he/she believes have income chargeable to tax, to file returns of income. However, omission to issue such notices does not exempt any perform from tax, as pointed earlier, such persons have the ultimate responsibility to declare their chargeability to tax by issuing a notice to the Commissioner that they are so chargeable.

In as far as notices of chargeability are concerned, the Commissioner is by law required to observe the statutory minimum period of thirty days from the date of service of notice.

It was held in the case of **AT v. CIT**[369] that a notice requiring a return to be submitted by taxpayers in less than the statutory minimum period is invalid *ab inition.* And even a subsequent extension of time does not validate such an invalid notice.

Assessment

The term "assessment" is defined in sub-section 2 (1) to mean "in any assessment or an additional assessment made under this Act." This definition lacks clarity. Assessment refers to all the procedures involved in the determination of tax liability. Assessment begins with the calling of returns of income, the determination of income assessable to tax, computation of the tax payable thereon and the imposition of the charge of tax on the income assessed.

After the returns of income have been submitted, the Commissioner will scrutinise returns to determine their reliability, and if satisfied, assess the taxpayer on the income disclosed in such returns.

---

368 Sub-section 78 (4)

369 2 EATC 370

Type of Assessments

There are about six types of assessments which can be made. These are, the normal assessment, estimated (or sometimes referred to as "presumptive") assessment, provisional assessment, estimated provisional assessment, jeorpady assessment and additional assessment. The general rule in sub-section 79 (1) is that, the Commissioner has an obligation to assess every person who has income chargeable to tax as expeditiously as possible after the expiry of the time allowed to such person under the Act for the delivery of a return of income.

a) *Normal Assessment*

This is an assessment made under sub-section 79 (2) (a) after due submission of a normal return. Such assessment is made after such return has been subjected to audit involving the examination of accounts and other documents to determine the return's reliability, for example, counter-checking such accounts and documents against previous records submitted to the Commissioner, visiting taxpayer's premises where it is considered necessary and such other things as may be necessary to verify the truthfulness of statements contained therein.

b) *Estimated Normal Assessment*

There are two instances where the Commissioner can raise estimated normal assessment. First under sub-section 79 (2) (b) where the return submitted in found to be unreliable. This happens if the Commissioner has reasonable cause to believe that such return is not true and correct. Second, under sub-section 79 (3) where no return has been submitted after the notice to submit has been served and the period for its submission has expired. In both instances the Commissioner is empowered to assess such taxpayers to "the best of his judgement."

The Best Judgement Rule

The phrase "best of his judgement" carries no statutory definition, but was judicially defined in the case of **Gunda Shubbayya v. CIT**[370]

---

[370] (1939) 7 ITR 21

to mean that the Commissioner must have material on which to base his assessments must not be capricious, and is not entitled to make a guess without evidence, in that, he must himself take steps to procure material for the purpose if it is not already in his possession. The Commissioner in this regard has power to call witnesses and can make his own enquiries.

Illustrative Cases

In **CIT v. AA**[18] the defendant having jailed to submit a return was assessed to tax on estimated income. Notice of assessment was served on him by post. No objection was made against the assessment. Neither was any appeal lodged. When the demand note for the tax was served the taxpayer disputed it. It was held that the taxpayer was liable on the tax assessed on estimated income.

In **CIT v. Gian Singh**[371] the defendant neglected to submit a return of income. The Commissioner assessed him to income tax on estimated income. He did not object or appeal against the assessment. Having jailed to pay the tax due after the demand note was served, the Commissioner sued him for the tax and penalties. The defendant claimed that the assessments were excessive.

The Court held that:

1) Assessments are final and conclusive unless they are varied on objection or appeal;
2) The obligation to deliver the return is on the taxpayer; and
3) The Commissioner may raise an estimated assessment in the absence of a return even though non-delivery of the return is due to circumstances such as being lost in the post.

Note, however, taxpayers must be given an opportunity to submit a return before valid estimated assessment can be made.

In the case of **Mandavia v. CIT**[372] the Appellant was assessable to income tax for the years of income 1943-51. He had not been

[371] 3 EATC 24

[372] 2 EATC 426

required to make a return for all that time. Subsequently he gave oral notice of his liability to the charge of income tax in respect of the period in question. In 1953 the Commissioner sent notice requiring him to submit returns. But prior to the time for making such returns had expired the Commissioner raised assessments on his estimated income subject to final adjustments under sub-section 71 (our section 71 (3)).

The Privy Council held that granting the taxpayer an opportunity to make a return is a condition precedent to assessment under section 71. Before making an assessment under section 71 the time allowed for submitting returns under section 59 (our section 57) must elapse otherwise the assessments will not have been validly made.

In **AT v. CIT**[373] the appellant had made no returns for the years of income 1952-55. The Commissioner sent him notice to submit returns in one month from the date of issuing notice. Such time was less than the statutory period. The Commissioner allowed an extension of time but no returns were submitted. Subsequently estimated assessments were made on each year of income for the period.

It was held that the notices requiring the returns of income were invalid as they did not give the appellant minimum statutory time in which to submit the returns. Further that a notice requiring a return to be submitted by a taxpayer in less than the statutory time is void *ab initio* and an extension will not cure the irregularity. The right to assess under section 71 (i.e. the current sub-section 79 (3)) arises from giving a valid notice requiring return under section 59 (the current sub-section 57 (2)). Therefore the estimated assessment by the Commissioner were held to be invalid.

Service of Notices

Section 135 provides for the methods of service of notices under the Act as well as proof of service notices. Notices can be served either by personal delivery, or leaving the notice at the taxpayer's usual or last known place of address, or by post. Where the latter method is

[373] 2 EATC 370

adopted, in the absence of proof to the contrary, service is deemed to have been effected:

i) Where it is sent to any place within Tanzania, ten days after the date of posting; and

ii) Where it is sent to a place outside Tanzania, service is effected at the time at which the notice would be delivered in the ordinary course of post.

In proving such service it is sufficient to prove that the envelope containing the notice or other document was properly addressed and was posted.[374]

c) ***Provisional Assessment***

The Commissioner has an obligation under section 80(1) to make provisional assessment as expeditiously as possible as soon as the time to file a provisional return expires.

A provisional assessment is some kind of self assessment whereby the taxpayer provisionally assesses his own tax liability. Under sub-section 80 (2) where a person has furnished a provisional return he shall be deemed to have been provisionally assessed on the basis of the estimates contained in such return. Provisional assessment is advantageous in several ways:

i) It expedites the assessment process by avoiding pile up of returns at the end of the year of income.

ii) It enables adjustments to be made before a final return is submitted to determine the ultimate tax liability.

iii) It provides a solution to delayed final returns for lack of competed accounts.

d) ***Estimated Provisional Assessment***

This is made under sub-section 80 (3) where a taxpayer who is required to submit a provisional return fails to do so. Again here the Commissioner shall assess him to the best of his judgement.

---

[374] Sub-section 135 (3)

In **X v. CIT**[375] it was held that estimated assessment does not affect the liability that has already accrued. That estimated assessments should not be regarded as a sanction or penalty but simply as an additional method of assessing income tax on an alternative method of assessment.

e) ***Jeopardy Assessment***

An assessment in jeopardy can be raised under section 81 where the Commissioner has reasonable cause to believe that any person is about to leave Tanzania, or has left Tanzania and his absence is likely to be permanent, and such person has not been assessed to tax. The Commissioner may under such circumstances determine the amount of income of such person according to the best of his judgement and assess him accordingly.

f) ***Additional Assessment***

In the process of assessment, certain income of a taxpayer may escape assessment or be under assessed. Under section 83 as read together with sub-section 95 (2) the Commissioner can raise an additional assessment.

For example, where a taxpayer's income was underestimated because no return was submitted, or where the return submitted was rejected for being unreliable, or where the Commissioner changes his appreciation of facts on which has based his previous assessment.

In the case of **Jones v. Mason Investment Ltd.**[376] the respondent, a real estate company, was for years treated as a holding company and, therefore, given management expenses relief. Later, on reviewing the activities of the company the tax authorities changed their view and treated it as a property dealing company. No new facts had come to light for the change of view, but there an additional assessment was raised.

The Court held that the discovery to warrant an additional assessment may be accomplished by a change in the appreciation of same facts. Therefore the additional assessment was correctly made.

---

[375] 2 EATC 39

[376] 43 TC 570

In the case of **Perkin v. Cattel,**[377] an additional assessment was made after the revenue authorities found that the four houses which were purchased subject to controlled tenancies by a taxpayer and later sold with vacant possession had not been bought as investments but in the course of trade. No new facts were relied upon for the change of view by the Revenue Authority but the court was satisfied that reasonable grounds existed for the change of view and, therefore, discovery was accomplished.

Other Procedural Requirements in Relation to Assessments

Notice of Assessment

After an assessment has been made on the income of a taxpayer, section 84 requires the Commissioner, in all cases except in the case of an accepted provisional assessment (under sub-section 80 (2), to serve a notice of assessment to the taxpayer. Such notice will state the amount of income assessed, the amount of tax payable and shall also inform the taxpayer of his/her right of objection or appeal under section 91.

Limitation Period

The limitation period for making assessments is seven years after the year of income to which the assessment relates except in the circumstances listed in the proviso to sub-section 85 (1), that is, there is no limitation period where any fraud or gross or wilful neglect has been committed.

Assessment Lists

After expiry of the time allowed for delivery of returns in respect of each year of income, the Commissioner is required, under section 86, to prepare a list of all persons assessed to tax in that particular year of income. The list shall contain:

a) Name and address of assessee;
b) Amount of income upon which assessment is made; and
c) The amount of tax payable.

---

[377] 48 TC 472

This list is admissible as evidence in any proceedings under the Act, whether civil or criminal, if certified by the Commissioner to be a true copy. Any extract from the list if so certified by the Commissioner is *prima facie* evidence of the matters stated therein.[378]

Errors in Assessment or Notices

An error, mistake or omission in the assessment, warrant or document issued under the Act, if such assessment, warrant or document is in substance and effect in conformity with or according to the intent and the meaning of the Act, cannot constitute a ground for quashing, or rendering void or voidable any such assessment, warrant or document.[379] For example, a mistake as to the name of the person assessed, erroneous description of any income or a variance between the assessment and the notice of assessment which is not likely to deceive or mislead any person affected by the assessment cannot operate to nullify any assessmentor constitute or ground to impeach on assessment.[380]

Finality of Assessment

Assessments have to have an end to facilitate and expedite smooth collection of taxes. Sub-section 95 (1) provides that an assessment shall be final and conclusive if:

a) No notice of objection has been given; and
b) Where notice of objection has been given:
   i) The assessment has been amended under section 92(2).
   ii) There is disputed assessment under section 92(3) but no appeal has been preferred.
   iii) The assessment has been finally determined on appeal.

---

[378] Sub-section 86 (2)

[379] Sub-section 87 (1)

[380] Sub-section 87 (2)

However, sub-section 95 (2) gives two exceptions to the finality rule, namely:

a) The Commissioner, despite the finality envisaged in sub-section 95 (1), can raise additional assessment for any year of income, provided that, in so doing he/she does not re-open any matter which has been determined on an appeal or an assessment for such year of income.

b) The Commissioner, may, however, raise an additional assessment which re-opens a matter which has been determined on appeal where fraud or wilful neglect has been committed by, or on behalf of, any person in connection with or in relation to tax for any year of income.[381]

Relief for Error

Where a person alleges that an assessment was excessive by reason of some error or mistake of fact in a return, he may, not later than seven years after the expiry of such year of income make an application to the Commissioner for relief.[382]

Upon receipt of the application the Commissioner may inquire into the matter, and if satisfied, grant relief by way of repayment as is reasonable and just.[383] However, no such relief can be granted if the claim is based on an error or mistake as to basis on which the liability of an applicant should have been computed if the return of income was made according to generally prevailing practice at the time such return of income was made.[384]

PAYMENT AND COLLECTION OF TAX

Sub-section 99 (1A) requires a person who submitted a normal return under section 57, which by law was required to be prepared and certified by an authorised auditor or an authorised accountant, to pay tax on the date on which such return is due to be submitted to the Commissioner.

---

[381] Sub-section 95 (2)

[382] Sub-section 98 (1)

[383] Sub-section 98 (2)

[384] See *proviso* sub-section 98 (2)

In other words the due date for payment of tax for such person is the date which he/she is required to, and actually submits his/her return. This provision applies to all companies and to partnership firms with income in excess of Shs. 1,500,000/=.

Under sub-section 99 (2), where the tax is charged in any assessment other than a provisional assessment, for example, normal assessment on an individuals or a firm with income less than Shs. 150,000/=, the tax shall be payable:

a) In the case of an individual, within thirty days from the date of service of the notice of assessment; and

b) In the case of any person other than an individual if the return is a normal return, submitted section 57 and the assessment was made under section 79 (i.e. normal assessment) before 31st March in the year following the year of income in respect of which the tax is charged, the whole tax shall be paid on or before 31st March in such following year of income; and

c) In all other cases, the tax shall be payable within thirty days from the date of service of notice of assessment.

d) Note that, in respect of estimated normal assessments made under sub-sections 79 (2) (b) and (3) and additional assessment under section 83, and the due date for payment of tax if the assessment had been made under sub-section 79 (2) (a) would have passed at the time of raising the estimated or additional assessment, the date for payment of tax shall be the date on which notice of assessment is served upon the taxpayer.

e) In the case of jeopardy assessment made under section 81, the Commissioner may serve a notice in writing upon the assessee requiring payment of the whole tax or any part thereof within such time as he may specify in such notice.

f) Where provisional assessment is made under section 80 after submission of a return by a person other than an individual, the whole of the tax charged is payable within three months from the end of the accounting period. In the case of estimated provisional assessment under sub-section 80 (3), however, the tax shall be payable within thirty days from the date of service of notice of assessment.

g) Sub-section 99 (4) provides that where a provisional assessment is made on an individual under section 80, the tax shall be payable in four equal instalments unless such provisional return is amended in which case time for payment shall be varied accordingly.

h) Where a company is being wound up, the due date for payment of tax is the date next before the date of the winding up order, or the resolution passed for the winding up of the company, whether or not assessments have been made before that date.[385]

i) Where there is a valid objection under section 91 and the assessment has not been finally determined:

    a) Where the tax would have been payable in accordance with sub-section 99 (2) and the balance thereof be paid in accordance with section 100.

    b) After determination of assessment if any amount is overpaid the amount so overpaid and deposited with the Commissioner shall be repaid under sections 112 and 112A.[386]

Sub-section 99 (7) empowers the Commissioner to extend the period for the payment of any tax and specify another due date. Where any tax remains unpaid on the due date, section 101 imposes an interest of 25% on the amount of tax which remains unpaid. The rate of interest is raised by 1.5% after every 6 months. An interest is also imposed under section 102 where the difference between provisional assessment and final assessment is more than 20%. The rate is 1.5% of the whole of the difference between the tax so estimated per month.

---

[385] Sub-section 99 (5)

[386] Sub-section 99 (6)

RECOVERY AND ENFORCEMENT OF TAX

Taxpayers are required to meet their tax liability by the due dates prescribed for tax payment as above. However, where a taxpayer defaults to remit payments as required by law there are three main methods which the Commissioner may use to recover such tax, namely: recovery by appointment of an agent; recoverly suit; and recoverly by distraint.

Recovery by Appointment of Agent

This method is provided for under section 103. Where the assessee has failed to pay the tax due, in practice, the Commissioner will issue a warning letter which may also serve as a demand note. After fourteen days of the service of the warning letter, the Commissioner may under sub-section 103 (2), by notice in writing, appoint any person an agent of the defaulter for the purposes of collection and recovery of the tax due.

For example, in the case of **BX v. CIT**[387] a tenant was appointed an agent for collection against the lessor. It was held that in such cases the Commissioner steps into the shoes of the taxpayer (i.e. subrogation), but can acquire no right which the taxpayer does not have.

The agency notice must specify the amount of tax to be collected and recovered. The agency notice may be served on the taxpayer's banker or debtor, who upon receipt of notice becomes agent of the taxpayer for collection and recover of the tax due.[388] The person appointed an agent is usually one who owes money to the taxpayer or is owed money by the taxpayer. For example, a tenant to the landlord, a debtor to a creditor, a banker to a customer.

If the agent has no money which he/she holds for the taxpayer he/she should notify the Commissioner, in writing, that he is unable to comply to the notice by reason of the lack of moneys held by, or due from him to the taxpayer.[389] If he/she fails to give such notice, the

---

[387] (1964) Vol. IV part I EATC at 234.

[388] Sub-section 103 (8)

[389] Sub-section 103 (4)

Commissioner will presume that he/she has money due from him/her to his/her principal i.e. the taxpayer, or he/she is holding moneys for him/her and thus proceed to recover the tax due directly from such agent as if he/she were the taxpayer.[390]

In effecting recovery by appointment of agent the Commissioner can under sub-section 103 (6) require any person to furnish a return showing any monies which he/she is holding, or is due to him/her from the taxpayer. Where on agent pays the tax due, he/she shall be treated to have acted with the authority of the taxpayer (as his/her principal) and thus be entitled to be indemnified by such taxpayer in respect of such payment.[391]

Recovery by Suit

After the date due for payment of tax, if the taxpayer still fails to comply with the notice of assessment, the Commissioner may file a suit against the taxpayer in a court of competent jurisdiction. In the proceedings thereof, the Commissioner need not adduce any evidence. A certificate issued by him/her giving the name and address of the taxpayer and the amount of tax due and payable is sufficient evidence that such tax is due and payable by the person mentioned therein. Note that the tax is recoverable by suit as a debt due to the government.[392]

Recovery by Distraint

This method may apply where the defaulting assessee owns substantial property. The procedure followed is thus:[393]

i) The taxpayer will be notified of the outstanding tax liability and be required to pay within a given period;

[390] Sub-section 103 (5)

[391] Sub-section 103 (8)

[392] See the provisions of section 108

[393] See section 109

ii) If he/she fails a bailiff is appointed under the **Income Tax (Distrant) Regulations, 1975**[394] to inquire into the residence and value of the property owned by the defaulter;

iii) Upon the findings of the bailiff the Commissioner appoints a destrain officer from among the section officers in the collection section;

iv) Then a warrant of destrain is served upon the defaulter and an inventory made of his/her assets;

v) Notice of distress is then issued in which the amount and value of the goods destrained are recorded and described;

vi) The taxpayer is then given ten days to pay the tax plus distress costs involved;

vii) At the expiry of the ten days period the destrain officer and the bailiff may sell the property by public auction to realise the amount outstanding and all incidental costs.

Note that, destrain procedure can be long, expensive and exposes officers to risk of violence and injury.

Other Enforcement Methods

a) *Collection from Estate*

Where a person dies and has not paid his/her tax due, the same shall be recovered as a debt due and payable out of his/her estate.[395]

b) *Requirement of Security*

Where a person is believed to be about to leave Tanzania or has left the country without paying his/her tax due, the Commissioner may under section 105, either:

i) Issue a notice in writing requiring such person to pay the tax charged within a specified time; or

---

[394] GN No. 7 of 1975

[395] Section 104

ii) Issue a notice requiring such person to give security for the payment of tax to his satisfaction.

Where a person fails to comply with any such notice served personally on him/her, the Commissioner may apply to a Resident Magistrate for the arrest of such person.[396] Such person will be brought to court to show cause why he/she should not pay the tax or give security to the satisfaction of the Commissioner. But, if such person pays the amount of tax due to the arresting officer he/she shall not be arrested.

If he/she fails to show cause and fails to discharge his/her tax liability the court may commit him/her to prison until either he/she pays the tax or furnishes security, provided that the detention in prison shall not exceed 6 months.[397]

c) ***Recovery from a Guarantor***

Where under sub-sections 105 (1) or (2) security is given for payment of tax in the form of a guarantee, the guarantor thereof is obliged to pay the tax in default of payment of tax in terms of the security.

d) ***Recovery from Carriers***

Carriers such as shipowners, charterer or air transport operators may sometimes be compelled to pay tax by refusal of clearance from any port or airport in Tanzania. This may happen if tax is recoverable by suit under section 108 and has been charged on any such carried. The procedure in such a case is for the Commissioner to issue a certificate containing the name of such person and the amount of tax due and payable to the proper officer of customs, who shall, on receipt of such certificate, refuse clearance from any part or airport to any ship or aircraft owned by such person until such tax has been paid.

RIGHTS OF THE TAXPAYER

A taxpayer has a right to dispute an assessment made by the Commissioner by way of objection and appeal.

---

[396] Sub-section 105 (4)

[397] Sub-section 105 (5)

Objections Against Assessment

After service of notice of assessment under section 84 the taxpayer may, by a notice in writing, lodge an objection disputing an assessment. However, such objection shall not be entertained unless and until either:

a) The tax not in dispute is paid; or

b) The tax deemed under sub-section 99 (6) to be not in dispute, or half the tax assessed, whichever is greater, is paid; or

c) The Commissioner allows no tax or a lesser tax to be paid.[398]

The Commissioner may exercise his/her discretionary powers (in respect of (c) above) under sub-section 91 (3) where;

i) The taxpayer is unable to pay due to hardship; or

ii) There is uncertainty on a question of law or fact involved in the dispute.

The objection will be valid as provided in sub-section 91 (4) if:

a) It is lodged or received within thirty days after notice of assessment is served. Late objection may be accepted where the taxpayer was unable to file an objection due to sickness, absence from the country or any other reasonable cause.[399] A rejection of late objection is appellable provided the whole of the tax assessed is paid first.[400]

b) It states precisely the grounds of the objection. The practice, however, is to state generally that the assessment is excessive or wrong in law or that it does not correspond to return submitted.

On receipt of a valid notice of objection the Commissioner may hear or receive any evidence relevant to the assessment and proceed to:

a) Amend the assessment in line with the objection. In which case he/she shall issue a notice of amended assessment; or

---

[398] Sub-section 91 (3)

[399] See proviso to sub-section 91 (4)

[400] Sub-section 91 (5)

b) Amend the assessment in the light of the objection and any further evidence adduced, according to the best of his/her judgement. In such a case, if the taxpayer agrees, he/she shall issue a notice of amended assessment in the lines agreed. Where the taxpayer further disagrees, he/she shall issue a notice of non-agreed amended assessment and advice the taxpayer of his/her right of appeal.[401]

The rationale for having a preliminary objection to the Commissioner is to enable parties to the dispute to review their respective positions and possibly arrive at an agreed assessment before intervention by appellate bodies. This procedure avoids litigation.

Appeals

Any person may appeal against the Commissioner's decision made under section 92 (as above) to a National Tax Appeals Board.[402] In order for the appeal to be entertainable, the appellant must have:

a) Given notice in writing to the Commissioner of his/her intention to appeal within thirty days after the date of service upon him/her of the notice of the Commissioner's decision as required by sub-section 92 (3); and

b) Lodges the appeal with the Appeals Board within forty-five days of the date of service upon him/her of the notice under sub-section 92 (3).

The National Tax Appeals Board

The Appeals Board is established under sub-section 89 (1). It is constituted by a Chairman (usually a Senior Resident Magistrate) and one or two vice-chairmen all appointed by the President, four other members appointed by the Minister from each region, and a secretary, who is not a member. The members appointed must have experience and capacity in commercial and financial matters.

---

[401] Sub-section 92 (1)

[402] This is established under section 89 and the procedure for appeal is set out in the *Income Tax (Appeals Boards) Rules, 1975* GN. 218 of 1975.

The Chairman and vice-chairmen move to every region, where together with the four members appointed from that region they for an Appeals Board for the region.

Rules governing the procedure before the Appeals Board are contained in the **Income Tax (Appeals Board) Rules, 1975.**[403]

The Tax Appeals Tribnunal

Appeals from the Appeals Board lie with the Appeals Tribunal established under section 90(1). The Commissioner or a taxpayer may under sub-section 93 (2) appeal to the Appeals tribunal against the decision of the Appeals Board.

The Appeals Tribunal is constituted by a Judge of the High Court of Tanzania and two assessors, one of whom must be an authorised auditor or an authorised accountant. In determining any appeal the judge is not bound by the opinion of the assessor but must require each of them to give an opinion on the matter or issue.

Procedure on Appeal to the Appeals Tribunal

The party wishing to appeal to the Tribunal must do so within thirty days after the date on which a notice of the decision of the Appeals Board is served upon him.

However, such aggrieved party must, first, within fifteen days after the date on which the notice of the decision of the Appeals Board was served upon him, give notice, in writing, to the other party to the original appeal.

All the documents of appeal as provided for in the **Income Tax (Appeals Trinunal) Rules, 1975**[404] must be filed within the said thirty days. Under section 93(4), however, a party may apply for an extension of time in which to give notice of appeal where no notice is issued as discussed above.

---

[403] (*Supra*)

[404] GN. No. 217 of 1975

Further, sub-section 93 (5) provides that, no appeal shall be entertained unless the appellant, before lodging the appeal, has deposited with the Commissioner the whole of the tax assessed under the assessment or amended assessment, plus any interest due under section 101, unless the Commissioner exempts such person from his/her requirement.

The appeal is preferred by way of a memorandum of appeal which shall:

a) Set forth the grounds of appeal;

b) Be signed by the appellant;

c) Accompanied by the confirming or amending notice or decision of the Appeals Board;

d) A statement of facts on which the appeal is based; and

e) A copy of the notice of appeal.

The Hearing

The appellant can appear before the appellate authority either in person or his/her duly authorised agent.[405] However, advocates can only appear before the Tribunal,[406] although they are not excluded from appearing before an Appeals Board. The law is merely silent on the issue. Thus an advocate may appear before the Appeals Board as an authorised agent.

In hearing the appeal the appellate authority may summon and hear witnesses and receive evidence in any manner and to the same extent as if it were a court exercising civil jurisdiction in a civil case and the provisions of the **Civil Procedure Code, 1966**[407] shall apply. However, in the case of a Tribunal, it may not admit fresh evidence save in the circumstances in which the High Court may admit fresh evidence on a first appeal in a civil case.[408]

---

[405] Section 94

[406] See proviso (ii) to section 94 (a)

[407] Act No. 49 of 1966

[408] See proviso to section 94 (b)

Powers on Appeal

The appellate authority may confirm, reduce, increase or annul the assessment concerned or make such other order as it thinks fit.[409] Within fifteen days of its decision such appellate authority shall issue and serve a notice of such decision on the parties.

The decision of the Tribunal shall be final and no appeal shall lie against that decision to any court or other authority.

---

[409] Section 94 (d)

12

OFFENCES, PENALTIES AND MISCELLANEOUS MATTERS

OFFENCES AND PENALTIES

In order to give effect to the provisions of the Act and ensure compliance therewith, the Act contains provisions for offences arising from infringement of the regulations contained therein, and prescribes penalties thereof. As it is usual with taxing legislation the penalties prescribed are often high in order to discourage taxpayers from indulgence into anti-tax activities.

General Provision Relating to Offences

Section 114 provides generally for offences. Under sub-section (1) thereof, a person guilty of a tax offence for which no other penalty is specifically provided shall be liable on conviction to a fine not exceeding fifty thousand shilling or incarceration for a term not exceeding two years or both such fine and incarceration.

Offences by Agents and Employees

Where an agent or employee is guilty of an offence both such agent or employee and his/her principal or employer are liable to prosecution.

The extension of liability here is intended to be a deterrent measure rather than a simple vicarious liability.[410]

Note that court of the Resident magistrates are empowered under sub-section 114 (3) to impose maximum penalties prescribed notwithstanding the limitation in their ordinary pecuniary jurisdiction.

Failure to Comply with Notice of Return

It is an offence for any person required by law to submit a return, to fail to submit such return, or to furnish a full and true return, or to fail to give notice of chargeability to the Commissioners, or not to keep and preserve records and books of account, or to fail to produce any document for the examination of the Commissioner or to destroy, damage or deface any accounts etc.[411]

Further, any person who without reasonable cause makes any incorrect return or furnishes incorrect information is also guilty or an offence.[412] And under section 118 any person who furnishes fraudulent returns shall be guilty of an offence and be liable on conviction to a fine not exceeding two hundred and fifty thousand or double the amount of tax for which he is liable whichever is greater or to imprisonment for a term not exceeding five years or to both such fine and imprisonment.

Obstruction

It is an offence under section 119 in any way to obstruct or attempt to obstruct an officer in the performance of his duties or exercise of his/ her powers under the Act.

MISCELLANEOUS MATTERS

Burden of Proof

The burden of proof in cases under the Act lies with the person charged.[413]

---

[410] Section 114 (2)

[411] Section 116

[412] Section 117

[413] Section 120

Power to Compound Offences

The Commissioner has power to compound any offence under the Act other than offences committed by officers of the Department in connection with their duties. The Commissioner, may, in such a case order the accused to pay any amount not exceeding one half of the amount of fine to which he would have been liable if he had been convicted of such offence.[414]

However, the Commissioner can only exercise such powers where the person concerned admits in writing that he has committed such offence. The Commissioner's order is appellable to the High Court within thirty days of such order being made.[415]

Place of Trial and Jurisdiction of Courts

Section 122 provides that, any person charged with any offence under the Act may be proceeded against, tried and punished, by any court in Tanganyika within the jurisdiction of which he may be in custody for that offence or to which he may be brought after arrest on a warrant issued by that court.

Other Powers of the Commissioner

The Commissioner has been conferred with enormous powers to enable the enforcement of the provisions of the Act. These range from powers of search and seizure[416] to powers to inspect books and documents.[417]

Note that, under section 124, any officer of the Department may appear and prosecute or tax case provided that, the Commissioner has, after due consultation with the Director of Public Prosecutions, in writing authorised such officer to conduct such prosecution. In tax cases of a civil nature, however, it is sufficient that the Commissioner authorises an officer in writing i.e. there is no requirement for the approval of the DPP.

---

[415] Sub-section 121 (3)

[416] Section 126

[417] Section 127

Effect of Conviction

The conviction of a person for a tax offence does not absolve such person from tax liability. The tax due and payable is still payable notwithstanding prosecution and conviction, and where a penalty or interest or both have been imposed, they are also payable.[418]

Set-Off of Tax

Any amount of tax which has been deducted by a person, for example, withholding tax under section 34, or by a trustee or trustees of a will or settlement under section 35, or by an employer under section 36, or which has been borne by any trustee in his capacity as such on any amount paid as income to any beneficiary, is usually treated as having been paid by the person chargeable with such tax.

Section 41 authorises the set-off for the purposes of collection against the tax charged on such person for the year of income in respect of which it was deducted.

Personal Reliefs

A taxpayer is entitled to claim certain specified reliefs from the Commissioner in respect of tax paid if:

a) Such person is a resident person; and

b) Has furnished all particulars and proof in respect of the relief claimed to the satisfaction of the Commissioner; and

c) Has furnished a return of income or provisional return of income or if such person is an employee his tax is being deducted by his employer under section 36.

The relief entitlement is on an annual basis. Therefore, where an individual taxpayer ceases to be resident, he automatically looses his right to relief, however, he shall be entitled to only a proportion of the reliefs granted which correspond to the number of months in a year of income in which he was resident.[419]

---

[418] Section 125

[419] See Part VIIIA

The relief which can be claimed is restricted to insurance relief. The insurance relief is available under section 32E to a resident individual who in any year of income:

i) Makes payments for insurance of his life or his spouse's life or that of his dependant child;

ii) Pays tax in respect of any amount of life insurance premiums payable by his employer on his life and which is included in his income under sub-section 5 (2) (b); and

iii) Makes current contributions to any approved pension or provident fund.

All these reliefs are given by way of a set-off of tax i.e. the relief granted is deducted against the tax payable by the grantee in that year of income. It is a tax credit.

www.ingramcontent.com/pod-product-compliance
Lightning Source LLC
La Vergne TN
LVHW052320200926
848481LV00002B/617